Martin Heald was a wireless operator in the RAF and now lives in Holland with his true life partner. The tale of his reincarnation was also told by the British TV series *Strange But True*. He relates the details of his extraordinary life in *Destiny*, his first book.

DESTINY

The True Story of One Man's Journey through Life, Death and Rebirth

MARTIN HEALD

E L E M E N T

Shaftesbury, Dorset • Rockport, Massachusetts
Melbourne, Victoria

First published in Great Britain in 1997 by
Element Books Limited
Shaftesbury, Dorset SP7 8BP

Published in the USA in 1997 by
Element Books, Inc.
PO Box 830, Rockport, MA 01966

Published in Australia in 1997 by
Element Books and distributed
by Penguin Books Australia Ltd
487 Maroondah Highway, Ringwood,
Victoria 3134

Cover illustration by J Catt
Cover design by Slatter & Anderson
Page design by Roger Lightfoot
Typeset by Footnote Graphics, Warminster, Wilts.
Printed and bound in Great Britain by Hartnolls Limited, Bodmin, Cornwall

British Library Cataloguing in Publication
data available

Library of Congress Cataloging in Publication
data available

ISBN 1 86204 129 6

ACKNOWLEDGEMENTS

First and foremost I would like to express my heartfelt gratitude to my partner Jen, for her unflinching love and support during the writing of this book.

I would also like to acknowledge the kind assistance of Saskia de Bruin, Josee van Asten, Roy Stemman, London Weekend Television, the van Leeuwen family and last, but by no means least, my publishers, Element Books.

INTRODUCTION

It is often difficult to make sense of our lives, even at the best of times. We seem to be swept along by the current of life at such a pace that we rarely have time to consider the reality of who we are or where we are going. If there is a greater plan or purpose to our existence, it escapes us. Occasionally, however, we may become aware of a certain pattern of events underlying our lives that obliges us to wake up from our daily routine to search for some kind of deeper meaning, whatever that may be.

The sequence of events that led me to embark on my own particular search was set in motion while I was still a very young child. At the time, of course, I was too young to be aware of their deeper significance. It is only in the last year or so that the various pieces of the puzzle have finally come together like a well-fitting jigsaw, thus making sense of the particular direction my life has taken up until now.

The experiences I describe in these pages are true, but my story is by no means unique. We all have a destiny to which we aspire, a 'book of life' that we are unconsciously writing each and every day of our lives. In writing my story I hope that others will be encouraged to set out to discover their own destiny. If you do set out on such a path, persevere. Don't give up at the first setback, for the final rewards will be worth more than anything money can buy.

ONE

One of my earliest childhood memories is of a holiday at the seaside. The journey took us through lush green meadows, where the sight of cows and sheep playing with their young was a completely new experience for a young town dweller. Our destination was Cleveleys, a small seaside town on the north-west coast of England. I will never forget that first glimpse of golden sand, bathed in the warm glow of a sunny midsummer's day. The sky seemed so much bluer and the air so much cleaner and fresher than in my home town. The most stunning aspect was the sea, with its blue and white waves crashing along the warm golden shoreline.

My father had wrestled with and finally set up the deck chairs, when I noticed a tractor and trailer giving people rides along the sand and into the sea. My father must have read my mind and in no time at all I was sitting on the back of the tractor, having the time of my life. It was such a thrill. I can still taste the salty tears that were shed as the ride came to an abrupt end.

I pestered my father for another ride, but he pointed out that the driver had gone home for his lunch. My heart sank. I wanted so much to experience those special few moments once again. I decided that the driver would return if he saw somebody waiting, so I asked my father if I could go and take a closer look at the tractor. He agreed, and I ran off as fast as my legs would carry me. As I looked back towards my parents, I could see them, complete with sunglasses, settling into the deck chairs, ready to soak up the warm midday sun. I continued towards my target, completely ignoring what appeared to be a small puddle of water in front of me. Before I'd realized what was happening, I'd plunged feet first into a deep hole dug into the sand, which by now had filled up with sea water. My feet touched the sandy bottom and it seemed that, no matter how hard I struggled, I couldn't regain the surface. I began to panic and took in two deep breaths, filling my lungs with cold, salty water, swiftly followed by the realization that I was going to die.

A tremendous feeling of peace came over me as the sunlight disappeared, leaving me in total darkness. I suddenly became aware of an extremely bright light in the distance which seemed to be approaching at an unbelievable speed. Instinctively I tried to close my eyes.

The next moment I found myself sitting in a small brightly lit room, along with several other people. The room closely resembled a doctor's waiting room and I was just about to ask one of the other people what was going on, when one of three doors opposite opened and a man bathed in an unbelievably beautiful light beckoned me to follow him. I entered the room and was just about to sit down on the floor, when the stranger introduced himself.

'Hello, Martin. I didn't expect to see you again so soon. It's me, David.'

'David?' I thought. 'I don't know anyone called David.'

'It doesn't really matter. You will remember me given time. You've just had an unplanned accident and drowned and now you must return and finish your life.'

I was about to protest when I felt a terrible pain in my chest. In an instant I was transported back to the beach, and found myself on the warm sand, coughing sea water out of my lungs. My parents were crying with relief. Back at our hotel, I was given a complete medical followed by a soothing cup of sweet, hot tea. I tried in vain to relate my story of David and the strange waiting room, but I was so weak from my ordeal that I soon fell into a deep and relaxing sleep. Since then I have tried on many occasions to tell the story to my parents, but without success.

My first day at school was an event I looked forward to, especially after hearing the description painted by my parents – learning, playing, not to mention making new friends. When the day arrived I was overcome with emotion, especially when my mother kissed me goodbye.

'I will be back later to pick you up,' she reassured me.

Sure enough, at the end of the day, there she stood at the school gates along with many other anxious parents. I cried once again, although more from relief that she had kept her promise to pick me up.

During my second week at school our teacher handed out new exercise books, together with pens and coloured pencils.

'Today, children, we are going to learn the first three letters of the alphabet. I want you all to copy A, B and C from the blackboard into your new books.'

My first thought was how boring and I began immediately on an intricate drawing, using all the brightly coloured pencils we had been given. I already know the entire alphabet, I thought to myself. Why should I be expected to copy out A, B and C? I can still recall the look of shock on the teacher's face when she saw what I was doing, not to mention her high-pitched scolding voice.

After a short time in the class I got the distinct impression that the teacher regarded me as a backward child, especially when I couldn't carry out the simple tasks she set us. She was soon to change her mind as, by the age of seven, I'd somehow developed the reading and writing age of an adult.

The headmaster soon realized my potential and suggested that I spend at least some part of the day receiving private tuition from him. Encouraged by teachers and parents alike, my artistic talents began to blossom.

I was so engrossed by my own development that I'd almost forgotten the new arrival to our family, my baby brother Andrew. However, the atmosphere and situation at home began to change and I was confronted with the realization that Andrew was getting more of our parents' attention than I was. I became quite jealous, flatly refusing to share anything with this 'intruder'. How dare he come and spoil everything! I am afraid that this resentment lasted until I reached adulthood when the situation became much clearer.

Apparently, my general health suffered during those early years, illnesses such as measles, mumps and chicken pox being then an integral part of childhood. In between my bouts of illness I used to spend some weekends at my grandparents, which gave my mother time to recharge her batteries for the week to follow.

I loved the company of my grandfather. He radiated a special kind of love and warmth and always took the time to try and answer some of the awkward questions that I put to him.

It was during one of these question and answer sessions that I asked him why he drank so much. As he was on the verge of replying, I added, 'Was it because of the war? Did you have to kill people?' His face turned a strange shade of grey as he replied, in a faltering voice, 'I don't want to discuss the war – it wasn't very nice – but when you are old enough I will make sure that you get my medals. How about that?'

After being safely tucked up into bed, I overheard my grandparents asking each other how such a young child could possibly know about the war . . .

Christmas was always an exciting time for my brother and me. The fact that we didn't have a lot of money didn't seem to make a scrap of difference. Our Christmas pillow cases were always full to the brim with toys and various goodies, guaranteed to keep us occupied for at least two weeks. I'd become conscious at an early age that Santa Claus didn't really exist and cruelly communicated this fact to my younger brother. One year, a few weeks before Christmas, we decided to have a good search in our parents' bedroom, for the 'presents from Santa Claus'. During one of these surreptitious search parties I inadvertently discovered a large box containing two field telephones. After a bit of cajoling, my father set the two telephones up between bedrooms and began to speak to me through the handset, explaining that if I wanted to reply I had to press the green button on the one that I held. My eyes were automatically drawn to a second, red button, along with a diagram consisting of the alphabet, followed by lots of strange dots and dashes. I immediately pressed the green button and asked my father what the strange diagram meant. 'Oh, that's Morse code,' he explained, and began to tap out SOS on the telephone. The bedroom faded. Within seconds I was floating high above the clouds, staring into the darkened night sky. Almost directly below my high vantage point I could see an aircraft being pursued by a much smaller and faster aircraft. Following a second attack, the larger aircraft exploded with a deafening roar, sending a jolt of terror through my already trembling body.

I was about to scream for help when the scene vanished just as quickly as it had appeared. I found myself back in the bedroom, listening to the Morse code. I tried to explain to my father what had just taken place, only to be laughed at and once again reminded about my daydreaming. From that moment on, I didn't dare to use the telephones for fear of returning to that terrible scene.

Another toy in our household was the record player. I was completely fascinated by this magical instrument. One evening my father decided to play an old Marlene Dietrich record sung in German. Stunned, I sat on the floor, listening to this strange but seemingly familiar foreign language, overwhelmed by scenes and emotions from a bygone era. After some persuasion my father agreed to buy me a German language course on a long-playing record, together with a German–English dictionary.

Academically, my education seemed to be going in the right direction, although I must admit to feeling rather bored during lessons. Most of the time I felt like an adult trapped in a child's body. I was quite good at sports, especially sprinting, and on quite a few occasions the teachers had to hold me back, to give the other children a chance to catch me, as by this time I had developed a strange sense of knowing exactly what my fellow pupils' next move would be. I couldn't understand this phenomenon, but soon realized its advantages, especially to a mischievous little six-year-old.

Playtime at school was the most exciting time of the day. One whole hour without those tediously boring lessons, giving my comrades and me plenty of time to explore the old air raid shelters. During one of our expeditions in the school grounds we came across an old outbuilding, completely destroyed apart from two small rooms. I'd just about managed to climb over the damaged window frame, when we were apprehended by one of the teachers.

'You mustn't go in there. This used to be part of the original school. It was bombed by the Germans during the war, killing some of the children and has remained as a memorial to this day.'

Once again I was overwhelmed with emotion, although by this time I was beginning to see the connection between these strange feelings and an event which had taken place years before I was even born.

At home everything was fine, although I still fought regularly with my brother, mostly without any logical reason. In an attempt to calm the situation down, we were given a set of old encyclopaedias which had belonged to my grandparents. These kept me occupied most of the time, as I had developed a thirst for 'real' knowledge. Whilst I was busy flipping through the pages of the seventh volume, the strange feeling returned to haunt me. I had reached the section headed 'Aviation in the Second World War' and there it was, the very same aircraft I had seen during that frightening vision. I read on, disregarding the feelings which had me trembling with a curious mixture of fear and elation. 'Morse code' – the Halifax bomber was usually manned by a crew of seven including the wireless operator who, by the use of Morse code, communicated to the home base during the long night-time bombing raids over Germany. The whole subject of the Second World War intrigued me, especially the feelings of recognition I experienced whilst flipping through pages of old photographs, taken during the war period.

At last I reached the age of model building. All my school friends seemed to be busy with model ships or cars, but my bedroom became filled with Halifax and Lancaster bombers, painstakingly constructed during the long school holidays. It was during one of these holidays that I heard the wailing of an air raid siren, signalling the workers' lunch break at one of the local factories. Every time the alarm sounded, a shiver ran through my body, followed swiftly by images of people rushing around the streets, their faces etched in panic, trying to reach the safety of an air raid shelter before the raid itself began.

Feelings of frustration and helplessness overcame me once again. I had given up trying to obtain a satisfactory explanation from my parents, who always seemed to put these episodes down to my vivid imagination. Imagination or not, the feelings and scenes were real enough to me.

On one occasion my brother and I were having what must have been our tenth argument of the day, when my father came home unexpectedly. He'd had an accident at work and had lost half of his right index finger and I remember wondering if his finger would ever grow back. Eventually, after a long recuperation period at home, he returned to work and finally received compensation money from the insurance company. He decided to take the family on a dream holiday to Guernsey.

'Where's Guernsey, is it near Blackpool?' I asked innocently.

'No, it's another country quite far away. We are going to fly there!' exclaimed my father excitedly.

When the day for departure arrived, all the suitcases were packed and we set off for the airport in a black cab. After completing the check-in procedure, we walked out on to one of the sight-seeing balconies. My father pointed out the aircraft that we were going to be flying in. I couldn't believe my eyes. There on the tarmac stood a rickety looking aircraft with four propellers. My heart sank. What I had imagined would be one great childhood adventure was rapidly turning into my worst nightmare. The look on my face must have given the game away.

'What's the matter?' enquired my father.

'What happens if we get shot at whilst we are flying?' I asked in all seriousness. My mother smiled nervously, as my father burst into fits of laughter. Eventually we boarded the aircraft and, although the flight itself seemed to last forever, it went quite smoothly, especially after I'd realized that my father was right about the war having ended and the chances of being shot at were nil.

Guernsey was a fantastic wonderland, especially for two young town dwellers. I remember that the sun shone every single day, a welcome change from rainy Manchester.

During one of our many excursions around the island, our search for a suitable picnic spot took us across one of the many ranges of sand dunes. After what felt like a day of hiking around this rough and hilly terrain, I caught a glimpse of what appeared to be an old coal bunker.

'Dad, what's that over there?' I asked curiously.

'Oh, it's one of the old German bunkers from the war,' replied my father. Within five minutes we'd reached the overgrown entrance and after a brief struggle my father managed to squeeze his way through, followed swiftly by two over-excited sons embarking on the adventure of a lifetime. Once inside, I experienced a strange sense of familiarity. The various corridors and tunnels seemed to go on forever and, of course, I wanted to explore every inch of them. After a short altercation, followed by tears of frustration, my father promised to take us to the war museum before the holiday ended.

Our visit to the museum turned out to be an extremely confusing and emotional experience for me. I seemed to know so much about the exhibits that I surprised even myself, as I couldn't recall reading about German war equipment in the old encyclopaedias. My father seemed to be at a loss for words, merely nodding at my seemingly knowledgeable statements. Not once did he ask me how or where I had acquired such knowledge about the war years. Not that I would have been able to provide any sort of satisfactory explanation, as most of my statements were immediately written off as childhood fantasy. From that moment on I began to realize that my so-called 'imagination' had begun to grow in complexity. Not only that, it belonged to the 'real world' and wasn't in any shape or form governed by fantasy. I began experimenting with my new-found toy and realized that I seemed to know when a certain person was going to visit our house. During one of my so-called 'fantasies', I blurted out to my mother, 'What time is Grandmother coming round today?'

'She isn't coming round today,' was the reply.

Two hours later my grandmother arrived, quite without warning, explaining that she was just passing through and had decided to call in for a cup of tea!

Similar predictions soon became second nature to me, although after a short while I decided to keep them to myself, especially after overhearing my parents discussing the situation. I remember hearing distinctly such phrases as 'not normal' and 'extra-sensory perception'. What on earth could that mean? I thought to myself. Was it perhaps some kind of terrible illness or disease; would I have to go into hospital? I decided that it would be in my own best interest to keep any further 'fantasies' to myself, not wishing to be sent away to hospital, away from my parents.

I remember asking one or two of my trusted school friends if such things had ever happened to them, only to be greeted either by roars of laughter or silent astonishment. I began to feel more and more isolated despite having many friends, and couldn't help but feel like an outcast. I had absolutely no one to turn to, no one who could possibly begin to understand my feelings, let alone my thoughts, although I sensed that things were about to change, this time for the better.

My ninth birthday was only a few months away when my parents called a family meeting.

'How would you like a new baby brother or sister?' my father asked us.

I was dumbstruck! After all, it had taken me nearly six years to get used to my brother! My line of confused thought was interrupted by a second and even greater bombshell. We would be moving house shortly, to make room for our new family member.

I think it probably took me two or three weeks to come to terms with the great changes that were about to take place. Saddest for me was the prospect of leaving school and all my friends. Would I ever have any friends again? I wondered. How on earth could I begin to make new friends?

With all these worrying thoughts filling my head we set off to visit our future home. After a short bus journey followed by a brisk walk, we had arrived. At first sight our new home didn't seem to differ too much from our present abode, until we ventured inside. The rooms seemed at least two or three times larger and the stairs leading to the bedrooms seemed to go on forever. It was breathtaking – three very large bedrooms plus the attic. I quickly came to the conclusion that this moving business wasn't going to be too bad after all. I had already chosen my bedroom to be, the attic, which although large offered me the privacy that, even then, I realized I would need.

The actual move was a complete blur. On the second day in our new home my brother and I began to get under our parents' feet and were told, in no uncertain terms, to 'go and play outside'. We had been playing football for about ten minutes when we were approached by a group of rough looking children. I picked up the football immediately, sensing danger. For once in my life I felt protective towards my brother and told him to run back home – I would be right behind him. No sooner had he turned to make a run for it than we came under attack.

My first black eye came as a bit of a shock, especially to my mother, although my father seemed to take it in his stride as he offered us well-meant advice about 'sticking up for yourself against bullies'. It's all very well for you, I thought bitterly. You're twice the size of those children and we were out-numbered by at least five to one.

It took me quite a while to get over that experience. Before then I had only seen scenes of violence on television and couldn't conceive such an unwarranted attack happening to me. The realization began to dawn that the world wasn't a bed of roses after all.

However, within a few short weeks of the incident, following various other initiations, we were finally accepted as part of the local scene. Just in time, too, as the new school term loomed menacingly. At least now I would have a few friends at the new school, although listening to their accounts of what awaited us I felt more than a little apprehensive.

The first day flew by, without any hint of trouble to follow. After a hurried introduction to my new classmates, I soon began to lose my initial shyness and started to question them about the sort of lessons that were taught.

'Yes,' I went on, with the innocence of a newly born infant. 'But what about art or painting?'

'That's for nancy boys,' replied one rather menacing-looking boy.

'Oh yes,' I agreed, thinking more of self-preservation than bravado; I would have plenty of time to make enemies, I thought, as the fourth fight begin in as many minutes. I hadn't given bullying in school a second thought, although I soon began to realize that my new school was a completely different kettle of fish to my previous one. The hierarchy was established from a very early age; each class had a 'best' fighter, who had his own second in command, as I was about to discover, to my cost!

'Hey, you over there, new boy, let's have your money,' shouted the best fighter in my class.

'No chance,' I replied, thinking how hard my father had worked for the few coins in my pocket.

'Oh, what have we got here then?' the boy went on.

I was just about to retreat when the school bell signalled my reprieve, or so I thought.

The first lesson of the afternoon had just started when the teacher left the classroom, explaining that she would be back shortly. How shortly? I wondered, a pit of fear rising from my stomach. She'd barely left the room when the taunts began.

'Hey, new boy, I'm going to have you,' the bully rasped, egged on by his fellow gang members.

Before I could think, the words had already tumbled out of my dry mouth. 'You don't think I'm scared of you, do you?'

Too late now I thought, as the first punches and kicks rained in on me. I grappled with the two bullies, desks and chairs flying in all directions. I tried to hold on to the teacher's table to remain upright, for fear of being kicked to death, but the table gave way and toppled over on top of the three of us. By this time the whole class was in complete disarray. Alerted by the bedlam, two teachers finally came to my rescue.

The headmaster dismissed my side of the events. 'There are no bullies in my school,' he shouted, as the leather strap came down against my stinging hand for the third time. I cried out, more in frustration than pain, and then made my way back to a now silent classroom. From that moment on I was regarded with great respect. Apparently, corporal punishment was regarded as the last resort, and anyone who survived this ultimate punishment became an instant hero. This sorry episode taught me one of life's tougher lessons – that before you can enjoy the fruits of your endeavours you must first experience the very lowest points in your life. It is then, and only then, that a person can truly appreciate the meaning of his or her own existence.

Without uttering a word to my parents about the day's traumatic events, I took refuge in my attic sanctuary. I lay on the bed staring blankly at the darkening ceiling and daydreaming about some of the incidents from my earlier childhood, especially the strange events connected with my 'fantasy'. Perhaps if I could show my friends a few of my earlier exploits, I would be accepted in this new environment. It wasn't long before the strange feelings returned, along with a number of coincidences which would give my life a totally different outlook.

TWO

My education now began to suffer, due mainly to boredom. This new school had none of the challenges or stimulation offered by my previous school. Mother, of course, soon noticed the difference. 'You should join the mobile library,' she suggested.

I walked dejectedly towards the mobile library van, knowing full well that the books designed for my age group would contain little or nothing of interest for me. I handed the signed consent form to the librarian who, after studying it, looked at me through horn-rimmed glasses, pointed to one small shelf and said, 'That section,' adding that the rest of the books were for adults only. I asked the librarian what 'adults only' meant.

'Sixteen years of age and over,' she replied brusquely, which was the adult manner of saying, shut up I'm very busy. I pretended to be interested in one of the books, until a group of younger children noisily entered the van. Now's my chance, I thought, and as quick as a flash began to sift through the so-called 'adult' section, without much success. I was about to leave when I spotted a shelf at the back end of the crowded van, proclaiming, OCCULT SECTION.

'Occult? What does that mean?' I wondered, thumbing through one of the books picked entirely at random. It was entitled *Extra-Sensory Perception: How to develop your own psychic abilities.* Extra-sensory perception I thought, my imagination running wild. I began to read the back cover as quickly as I could, being careful not to be seen by the librarian. Extra-sensory perception. The ability to read other people's thoughts and, 'Hey!' I'd been caught. 'Put that book back,' said the librarian. 'I've told you, that section over there is for you. If you don't want to borrow a book, then go away and stop wasting my time!' I left the library hurriedly.

By this time my imagination was working overtime. How could I possibly lay my hands on that book? It was tailor-made for me it seemed, using those same words mentioned by my parents all those years ago. I spent the rest of the evening trying to work out how I could get hold of it. It became a complete obsession. I *had* to have it.

But something else soon occupied my mind – the final examinations, which would decide the level of education we were to receive at secondary school. Having just got used to my new school, I was to be moved on once again. The large choice of secondary schools in our area soon resulted in a conflict between my mother and me. Most of my classmates had opted for the nearest school, which was within walking distance of our house. My mother had other ideas, as that school seemed to cater more for the sportsman than the academic student.

'I've invited Valerie round tomorrow evening, so that she can give you an idea or two about the school she attends,' said my mother triumphantly. I protested of course, to no avail!

Valerie duly arrived the following evening. To my surprise, my mother suggested that I show Valerie my bedroom whilst discussing the new school. I was in a complete panic. Valerie was much older than me, nearly sixteen, coupled with the fact that no girl had visited my sanctuary. What on earth was my mother playing at? Was she trying to embarrass me or trying to play matchmaker?

'Take your time,' echoed my mother's voice, just as I had reached the top step of the attic stairs. I turned around to make sure Valerie was following and couldn't help but catch a glimpse of her more than ample chest. My reddening face must have given me away, although Valerie didn't seem to notice.

'Well here we are,' I managed to say, almost stuttering with nervousness. 'Have a seat.'

Valerie immediately flopped down on to my bed and said, 'OK, what do you want to know?'

'Sorry!'

'About the school.'

'Oh yes, the school.' I replied, coming down to earth with a bump.

After a ten-minute-long question and answer session about the school I was still sceptical, until Valerie asked if I read any books or not.

'Well, I used to read a great deal when I was younger but . . .'

'Ever heard of the occult?' she interrupted.

The 'occult' – that very same word used in the mobile library. Throwing caution to the wind, I asked Valerie if she wouldn't mind obtaining my special book from the library.

'No problem. When do you want it?'

'Yesterday,' I replied jokingly.

'OK, if you write down the title for me, I will pick it up for you next week,' she said, adding a word of caution about not letting my parents ever catch me with it.

'Well?' enquired my mother.

'Well what?'

'The new school, have you made up your mind?'

'Yes, I've decided to go to the same school as Valerie.'

'That's marvellous.'

'I hope so,' I replied, playing along with the charade, whilst at the same time feeling ecstatic. At least I had met someone who not only seemed to understand my needs, but was also prepared to help, even at the risk of being caught.

The next week seemed to last forever. I tried to busy myself studying for the school exams. When the evening Valerie was due to come arrived, I sat in my room watching the street below, ready to sprint down two flights of stairs to the front door to make absolutely sure that I would answer it first, as she had instructed. I saw her coming and ran down, reaching the front door just as the sound of the doorbell reverberated through the house.

'Well, did you?'

'Shhhh,' scolded Valerie, handing me a plastic bag containing not one but three books. 'Yes,' she whispered, 'plus two other books, that I'm sure you will find more than interesting.'

I thanked her profusely, and arranged to return the books to her the following week.

'Are you sure that's enough time?'

'Plenty,' I replied, knowing full well that I would finish the books in two or three evenings. My curiosity seemed to take on a new dimension, probably due to the stealth being used to bypass unsuspecting parents.

'Who was that?' called my mother.

'Oh, it was Valerie asking about my choice of school.'

Quickly I ran up the stairs, being careful not to stumble and give the game away. Made it, I thought, locking the attic door, effectively shutting out the outside world.

I opened the first book, devouring it page by page. Psycho-kinesis, the ability to move inanimate objects using the power of your mind. The book was a mine of information, with detailed diagrams on how best to begin your own home experiments, utilizing everyday household items. The importance of keeping an up-to-date diary became patently obvious, not only for reference purposes, but to compare your own results against those contained in the book.

I could not believe what I was reading. This was a dream come true. Some of the strived-for results mentioned in the book bore a strong resemblance to my own childhood experiences, although the people quoted in the book were all adults, who had been practising for years. Why me? I thought, recalling the way I had been treated by my childhood friends. Despite these somewhat troubling thoughts, I really seemed to have no choice in the matter. The more I read, the more I wanted to know.

My newly acquired diary soon began to fill up with diagrams and experiments, ready to try out at the first opportunity. After a while I decided to get a paper round, which would enable me to buy the books I needed, instead of having to copy everything out into my diary, a cumbersome task at the best of times.

In my excitement I had all but forgotten my mother's preg-nancy, until one day while I was playing football in the school playground, my father arrived unexpectedly.

I ran towards him. 'What's the matter?'

'Your baby sister arrived a few hours ago. How would you like the afternoon off school to come and see her?'

Of course he didn't have to ask twice. Ten minutes later there we were, father, brother and I on the short bus journey, heading towards the hospital and my new sister.

The overpowering smell of disinfectant was soon forgotten as I held my new baby sister for the first time. It felt like holding a miracle, such a tiny human being, all within nine months. How could this be possible, this new creation?

The next few days were completely chaotic around the house, my father being at home for once. It took a while to get used to the situation, especially as I was expected to help with the preparations for the homecoming of my mother and sister. We just about managed to refurnish the small box room, which would eventually become my sister's bedroom.

The homecoming itself was an anticlimax for my brother and me. We were almost forgotten amongst all our visiting relatives and friends. The next few months were no less hectic, due mainly to the seemingly constant crying from my sister. For me, one good aspect about our new family addition was the fact that my parents were now so preoccupied that they hadn't even noticed my transformation. Instead of evenings spent playing football, my time was devoted to the various experiments and meditation exercises described in my slowly expanding library of books, although the chances of a successful meditation were very slim, due to the constant noise downstairs.

During this hectic period time flew by. I was soon saying another set of farewells to school friends and looking forward to starting my new secondary school. I would at least have a chance to see Valerie, as she had decided to stay on at school for one extra term in an attempt, I think, to avert the inevitable, the real world, with all its trials and tribulations.

I was placed in the intermediate level at my new school. This suited me down to the ground, as I seemed to be streets ahead of the rest of my fellow pupils. The first year flew by and, before I knew it, I had been placed in the higher class for my second year.

'Martin is wasting his time at this present level,' explained a well-meaning teacher to my parents. 'He definitely needs the challenge of a higher level of education.'

I wasn't so sure. At the present level I seemed to excel. The homework was relatively easy and definitely lighter than the homework received by the pupils at the higher level. My overriding concern was to make sure that I had enough time for my own studies. By comparison the school lessons paled into insignificance, in particular lessons involving physics or biology. To my mind, many of the books on those subjects seemed to be flawed and didn't reveal the truth about our planet, our evolution and last (but not least) the so-called 'paranormal', which was never mentioned by the teachers or in the school books. It felt to me like one enormous conspiracy to mislead us. Why keep such important subjects under wraps?

My head would pound with frustration, listening to the physics teacher's endless talk about Einstein and about Newton's theories, until, during one particularly detailed lesson, I couldn't hold back any longer and asked the teacher about psychokinesis. The whole class fell silent. There was a pregnant pause.

'Psychokinesis?' repeated the teacher. 'You mean people like Uri Geller, bending spoons and forks?'

'Yes,' I ventured, a little nervously.

The teacher burst out laughing, along with the rest of the class, and explained that Uri Geller was an illusionist who tricked people into believing that such feats were possible. I decided against carrying on with the conversation, as my new nickname was now being chanted by the majority of the class, 'Uri, Uri, Uri!'

By this time, I had reached adolescence and suddenly became interested in the opposite sex, although every attempt to make a meaningful contact with the local girls of my own age seemed doomed to failure. I began to wonder what I had to do to make myself more appealing when, out of the blue, one of my friends paid me an unexpected visit.

'Hi Martin, do you fancy joining the local scout group?' he asked. Before I had a chance to reply he added, 'Just think of it – a fantastic uniform, the chance to learn new things and go on camping trips, not to mention the posing. We are sure to attract the local girls.' I didn't have to think twice, as I'd always been fascinated by uniforms.

I was popular with the other scouts and within no time at all was promoted to the rank of patrol leader. But the novelty soon began to wear off and I left the troop. I remember pleading with the scout leader to let me keep the badges I had worked so hard for. My parents were naturally disappointed by my decision, especially as this meant more time for getting into trouble on the streets, mainly due to my built-up frustrations, which eventually erupted into violence.

My fascination with uniforms continued, however, and at the age of fourteen I decided to join the army cadets, despite the objections from my mother. 'It will make a man of him and also keep him off the streets,' explained my father.

The cadet uniform was far more professional-looking than that of the scouts and not very different from the regular army uniform. But the first few evenings in the army cadets were quite boring, spending hours learning the various drills and commands, whilst marching around the drill hall. And then came something that was to prove to be far more interesting. Rifle drill, followed by a live firing session on the specially built indoor rifle range. My excitement was compounded by the fact that I'd never even seen a rifle before, let alone fired one!

I watched as, one by one, my fellow cadets took their places on the mats, ready to fire. Barely a few seconds had elapsed from the first salvo, when it happened. The whole room took on a very different scenario, that belonged to a time and place gone by. Old-fashioned blue air force uniforms replaced the army olive greens; a stern-looking man, complete with handlebar moustache, was barking orders to the four men: 'Palmer, Jones Rankin and Seymour, move yourselves, we haven't got all bloody day, you know!'

I was about to panic when the drill sergeant's bellow interrupted my 'daydream'. I jumped.

'OK next four, come on we haven't got all bloody night you know.'

The words sent a frightening chill down my spine. I loaded the rifle and, on the sergeant's command, began to fire at the target. After we'd finished, it was time for a welcome cup of regulation army tea, while the bombardier counted up the scores from the shooting session.

'Heald, where's Heald?' bellowed the sergeant.

'Here, sergeant.'

'Have you been on the range before?'

'No, sergeant.'

'How do you explain this then, all ten shots in the bullseye?'

'Beginner's luck,' I replied, as he handed me the first badge of my new army cadet career, the marksman's badge.

The strange occurence was still in my mind during the short bus journey home. I had already decided against calling on Valerie, in case her mother answered the door. I finally arrived home to a dark and silent house, prepared my school books and went to bed. I must have lain there in the semi-darkness for more than an hour, trying to put the evening's strange events out of my mind, without success.

I reached over and switched on my bedside lamp. After a quick search under my bed, I found what I was looking for: *The A to Z of the Paranormal*. Surely I would find an answer to the peculiar events in this book. After ten minutes of feverish reading, I reached the letter O for Oracles. 'Ouija board, a modern oracle, comprising varnished wooden board, marked out with the letters of the alphabet, numbered from one to zero, together with the words yes and no.' According to the book, one was able to communicate with the spirit world using such a board. I knew instinctively that this was the answer I had been waiting for and remembered seeing one of these boards for sale in a local games store.

I saved hard for three weeks until, money jingling in my jeans' pocket, I set off towards the games store. I must have paced around the store at least three times, being very careful not to look directly at the board. I finally plucked up enough courage to approach the smiling shop assistant.

'Can I help you?'

'Yes, could you tell me how much this particular game costs?'

'You mean the Ouija board?'

'Yes,' I stammered, trying to remain calm.

'One pound 75 pence, but I must warn you, it isn't a game. You'd be playing with fire if you ever used it.'

'Yes I realize that,' I replied, beginning to lose heart. 'But it's for a friend's birthday.'

'Bring it over here. I'll wrap it up for you.'

'Brilliant,' I said, handing over my hard-earned cash. I was just about to leave the shop when the assistant added, 'If you have nightmares, I didn't sell it to you, OK?'

She obviously hadn't believed a word I'd said.

I breathed a gigantic sigh of relief once the attic door was firmly locked behind me. After quickly checking the instructions, I began my nervous chanting.

'Is there anybody there, is there anybody there?'

My fingers were shaking with anticipation, waiting for that fateful moment when, according to the instructions, the pointer would slowly begin to glide across the board and point to the word YES, signalling my first spiritual contact.

After a frustrating 20 minutes or so, my mother's voice interrupted my concentration, 'Martin, your tea is ready'. I carefully rewrapped my new toy, making sure it was well camouflaged under the bed, deciding to give it another go at a more opportune moment, perhaps with one of my friends.

Apparently spiritual contact is simplified if two or more people participate.

The school holidays were about to begin, and I had still made no contacts using the Ouija board by myself. The following week I was presented with a perfect opportunity – both mother and father working and brother and sister visiting grandparents. I'd already planned my strategy, inviting two of the toughest children from the neighbourhood, knowing full well that they wouldn't dare to refuse, for fear of losing face amongst their cronies.

Three days and a whole lot of organizing later, there we were, the three of us, sat around the circular dining table. It was quickly decided that I would take charge, as it was my 'game'.

'Is there anybody there?' I asked in all seriousness, to muffled laughter from my two guests. Ten frustrating minutes later, I was about to call it a day when it happened. I hadn't even finished my question when the pointer came to life, moving slowly across the board until it reached YES. Accusations began to fly.

'You pushed it!'

'No I didn't, it was you.'

'Quiet!' I shouted triumphantly.

'What is your name?'

The pointer immediately assumed a life of its own, criss-crossing smoothly across the board, finally spelling out the name DAVID FRENCH.

'Is this your real name?' I asked.

Once again the pointer sprang into action, YES.

My guests were suddenly stunned into silence, realizing that this was no longer a game.

'Shall we stop now, Martin?' asked one of them.

'No way, it's taken me a long time and effort to reach this stage.'

'How did you die, David?'

The pointer glided around the board like a ballerina on ice, spelling out, CAR CRASH. That's interesting, I thought.

'When did you die?'

Within ten minutes I had all the information that I needed: the boy's name, date of birth and death, followed by a London telephone number. I decided to end the session and thanked 'David' for his cooperation. After cups of tea, my friends persuaded me to try the telephone number. Why not? I thought. What have I got to lose?

The telephone at the other end began to ring. After the fifth ring a woman's voice repeated the number and said 'Hello'. I was completely shocked; in all the excitement, I hadn't even thought what I was going to say.

'Oh hello, could I speak to David, please?' I asked, as calmly as I could, under the circumstances. There was a moment of silence, broken by the sound of heart-rending tears, as the telephone at the other end was dropped. A different, male voice came down the telephone. 'Please, just leave us alone. We've already spoken to the press about David's accident.' I was just about to offer my condolences, when the line went dead.

My two comrades were by this time ready to leave and after promising not to breathe a word about the afternoon's events, hurried away, out of my life, although I did not know this then.

I should have known better than to trust two of the toughest boys in the area. Two days later, the father of one of them stood at the front door, relaying his version of the events to my mother. I hadn't even reached the attic door as my mother called out from below, 'Martin, get down the stairs'.

I felt a sense of panic, realizing that the game was up, and made my way down the stairs.

'Where is it?' My mother was visibly annoyed. I retrieved my pride and joy from its previously safe hiding place. She snatched the board from my trembling hands.

'This is going in the dustbin, where it belongs. I thought that you of all people had more sense than to dabble with such an evil devilish thing.'

After my mother had calmed down, I managed to persuade her not to inform my father. 'As long as you promise not to meddle with such dangerous things in the future. I'm at a loss to think where you get these ideas from. Why can't you act like the other normal children of your age?'

The words of admonishment were still ringing in my ears as I lay on my bed, relieved that my mother had discovered only the Ouija board. I came to the conclusion that from then on I would have to be extra cautious, keeping all my experiments and the results that followed to myself.

Two weeks had passed since the unfortunate incident, my Ouija board long since gone. Probably buried by now in some rubbish tip, I thought depressingly, while reading one of my newly acquired books on psychokinesis.

I decided to try out the first experiment to see if I'd lost my touch. Following the instructions carefully, I filled a bowl two-thirds with water and, after selecting a needle from my mother's sewing box, managed (after the third attempt) to float the needle on the water's surface. 'Meditate for five minutes, strongly visualizing a bright ball of energy above your head, hold your hand approximately five centimetres above the floating needle, simultaneously forcing the energy down your arm and out through the hand. Command the needle to move in any direction you will. Try not to worry if, on your first attempt, nothing happens – remember, practice makes perfect!'

Ten tiring minutes later, legs full of cramp, I was just about to call it a day when the needle began to move across the water-filled bowl. I was overjoyed and spent the rest of the afternoon making sure that I could repeat the result. I carefully noted the day's events in my diary, together with my own thoughts and feelings associated with the experiment, as I had read that one's mood before, during and after an experiment could have a significant effect on the outcome. Apparently the amount of usable energy created while in a good frame of mind is far greater and more powerful than the negative energy associated with sadness or depression. I decided to test the theory out in the future, should I have the chance.

I didn't have too long to wait to test the theory, as my beloved grandfather, who was by this time separated from my grand-mother and living alone, died suddenly in his sleep. This was my first experience of death in the family, and I just didn't know how to react. On the one hand, logical reasoning told me that I would never see my grandfather again; on the other hand, I was certain that the spirit of my grandfather lived on and would be able to find the peace and happiness that had always seemed to elude him, whilst he was alive.

Three weeks after my grandfather's funeral, the sad scenes of grief had taken their toll. I lay on my bed staring through tear-filled eyes at a family photograph album, showing the happier days of my grandfather's life, and wishing that I'd had one last chance to speak to him, to say a more personal goodbye. I must have dozed off to sleep, waking up with a start in the middle of the night. I couldn't believe my eyes! There he was, standing in the middle of my attic floor surrounded by a bright silvery-white light.

'Hello Martin, you don't have to worry about me any more. I'm living in God's kingdom now. No more alcohol for me, it's so beautiful and peaceful,' he said with a smile. 'One more thing before I go – you will receive my medals very shortly, as instructed in my will.'

'Goodbye grandfather,' I whispered, tears of happiness running down my cheeks. He had remembered his promise, made all those years ago. I closed my eyes, not doubting for one moment the reality of my wonderful experience. Two weeks later my grandmother arrived, to present me with the medals.

'Look after them,' she added, as she said a tearful goodbye.

I carefully opened the old metal box and could scarcely believe my eyes – 11 gleaming medals, won for bravery and courage shown against the enemy, sometimes against overwhelming odds.

The strange occurrences and coincidences in my life made me realize that I was different from most of the people around me. I felt as though my life had a special purpose, although I couldn't seem to pinpoint this purpose, mainly due to my ever-increasing ego. I could sense, see, hear and feel so much more than the normal human being. I was so preoccupied with my own little world, however, that I was completely unprepared for the tragedies that were soon to follow.

A little over three months had passed since my grandfather's sudden death. We were at the table and the dinner plates were being collected by my mother, just as the telephone began to ring. A strange feeling of sadness and loss invaded my thoughts, heralding the arrival of bad news. My father answered the telephone and after a short conversation, replaced the receiver and made his way into the kitchen, closing the door behind him. A few minutes later he put his head around the door. 'See you tomorrow night. I'm just going to visit your uncle in hospital.'

I questioned my mother on my father's sudden disappearance. 'Well,' she began, confirming my worst fears. 'Your uncle is very poorly at the moment.'

My uncle died that very same evening.

Three more tragedies were to befall our family within a terrible twelve-month period. My father's remaining brother died, my mother's mother died of a heart attack, then my father's mother also died. I seemed to slip into a sort of dream world where reality ceased to exist. At the time, this was the only manner I could think of to try and survive the reality of this terrible and heartbreaking situation. Not once did I see my father cry or hear him complain. He threw himself into his work as an engineer, until one day, overworked and totally exhausted, he ended up in hospital to have a hernia operation. The operation seemed to be a success until, six weeks later, on the doctor's advice, he was re-admitted for an exploratory operation, to try and find out why he hadn't fully recovered from such a simple operation.

Two weeks later he was sent home to convalesce, or so I thought until one day my brother and I arrived home unexpectedly from the local park. I heard the distinct sound of crying coming from my parents' bedroom. The truth hit me like a bolt of lightning, as I looked into my mother's tearful eyes.

'Does it begin with the letter D?' I asked, conscious of impending death and by this time fully aware of the situation.

'What on earth are we going to do?' sobbed my mother. 'How will we survive?'

For the next few weeks I moved around the house like a zombie, finally deciding to spend as much time as possible with my father. My world had slowly but surely begun to collapse. Here was the person I loved most dying before my very eyes, wasting away day by day, week by week, until that final merciful release.

My mother and I quickly worked out a shift system to look after my father, who, by this time, was living and sleeping downstairs, full of pain. I would sleep downstairs with him for a week, then it was my mother's turn. This allowed time to recover between our stints at this heart-rending task.

The morphine injections increased in strength and frequency, signalling that the end of my father's painful suffering was near.

My mother had started her shift, after a particularly distressing week for me. Within five minutes I had fallen into a deep dreamless sleep, only to be disturbed by the sound of muffled voices downstairs. I was just about to get out of bed to investigate, when one corner of my bedroom was suddenly illuminated by the same strangely bright light that had accompanied my grandfather's appearance. I couldn't move, my whole body refused to function, as I stared at this light. The next moment will remain with me for the rest of my life. Three hazy figures ascended into the light, then there he was, my father flanked by his two brothers, all smiling happily and looking much younger than they had when they were alive.

'Don't worry about me, Martin. I'm completely free of pain now. Promise me that you will look after your mother for me – she's going to need you more than ever now.'

'I will, Father, I promise,' I replied, as the three brothers continued their ascent, finally disappearing through my bedroom ceiling. I went back to sleep almost immediately, exhausted. The next morning I woke up hoping that my vision was nothing more than a dream. The uncontrollable sobbing downstairs soon confirmed the sad reality. How could I even begin to doubt these visions when to me they were more substantial than reality itself? I went downstairs and fell into my mother's arms as she began to stroke the cold waxy face of my father, whose long painful ordeal was now over.

The funeral was as blurred to me as the previous terrible twelve months had been. It was a deadly domino effect, first one relative, then another and then, before I knew it, I was attending my father's funeral. After three weeks away from school my mother decided that it was time for me to return.

'I understand exactly how you feel, but you can't postpone it forever. You've got to face up to reality.'

Reality, I thought – my reality was seven months left at school, without a hope of achieving any sort of decent examination results, due to my obsessive preoccupation with the occult.

As examination time loomed I began to take a serious look at my life so far. Yes, I thought, I've been lucky enough to be gifted with these extra talents, but what has that brought me? Nothing but trouble, lies, deception and a school education that I had absolutely no chance of rescuing. How could one make up three years of lost study time in three months?

I began to question God about the tragedies in my life. If I was so special, why did he allow these tragedies to occur? I swore repeatedly, cursing a god who could, at the drop of a hat, take away most of our family. Here my logic failed me. If my relatives, in my eyes such good-hearted law-abiding citizens, had to die so young, then maybe the good side of life wasn't worth pursuing after all.

My life began to take on a different meaning. I was changing from a quietly spoken, reasonable and sensible person, into a short-tempered and violent young man. Just as my mother needed me most, I seemed to be slipping further and further into oblivion, my library rapidly being filled with books of a darker nature. In a perverted way I was doing my best to get even with God the Creator.

THREE

The atmosphere in our once peaceful and loving home had been transformed into one full of arguments, swearing and the constant threat of violence. The school examinations were finished and I had started my last week at school when I was suddenly confronted by an ultimatum from my mother.

'Either you find a job immediately, or you're out of this house.'

I suppose such statements are meant well, but to me it signalled that the competition between God and myself was just beginning to hot up. Every evening before I fell asleep I used to curse Him, holding a sort of competition scoreline. I was determined to win, against all the odds, and I remember quietly celebrating the offer of a job as a warehouse assistant in the town, starting the following Monday. Yes, God, I thought to myself, you tried to have me thrown out of my house and failed miserably.

'That's another one to me!' I shouted, marking the new scoreline in my new black book, which by this stage was beginning to fill up quite nicely.

Throughout this tragic period my experiments in the paranormal began to take on a more sinister appearance, with the use of black candles and as much of the paraphernalia I could lay my hands on, depending entirely upon my financial situation. I'd found a mail order business willing to supply the necessary equipment without asking any awkward questions.

Yes, I thought, most people spend their lives expounding the theory that honesty is the best policy and that good will always triumph over evil, yet at the sight of money their morals melt away like snow.

I found my new job tedious and boring, once the initial challenge of being accepted into an adult environment had passed. This led me to question myself yet again about my very unsure future. What on earth was I going to do? I certainly wasn't going to stay in my present occupation as a labourer, that much I knew.

Christmas came and went, but it had lost its significance entirely due to, amongst other things, the loss of my father. I soon came to the conclusion that my destiny lay in my own hands. Not wishing to spend the rest of my life as a labourer, I finally decided to consult my own extensive library. I spent two weeks reading as many books as possible, hoping to find a way out of my depressing situation. I suddenly realized that since my father's death I hadn't had any more visions of *déjà vu* experience, which usually offered a way out of a difficult situation or, at the very least, a new insight. Could it have anything to do with the fact that I'd turned my back on God? I wondered, immediately deciding to make my peace with God, to see if my situation would in any way better itself.

Within three short weeks, I had the first sign, although I didn't realize it at the time. The house next door to ours had been up for sale for a while; suddenly the For Sale sign disappeared and the new neighbours moved in.

'You'll probably know our new neighbours,' my mother informed me. 'He went to the same school as you.'

Ten minutes later, unable to hold back my curiosity, I rang the front doorbell of the house next door, the door swung open and there stood one of my old classmates from the first year at secondary school. After introducing me to his family he suggested that we listen to his new records. We spoke at length about our old school, until finally reaching the subject of work.

'You're wasting your time there,' he said, and began to paint the most wonderful picture of his own job. 'Very relaxed atmosphere, lots of women, good pay and, what's more, it's within cycling distance!' he added, as a clincher. My face must have revealed my feelings.

'Don't worry, I'm well in with the boss. I could put in a good word for you, if you wanted.'

'That would be fantastic.' I had to raise my voice over the loud music, not expecting for one moment that he would.

* * *

Two weeks and one interview later, having said goodbye to my former workmates, I started my 'dream' job, in an old-fashioned weaving mill that seemed left over from the last century, although I wasn't complaining. My wages had doubled, there were no more bus fares to pay and, best of all, I was surrounded by women. I could scarcely believe my luck. Less than three weeks ago I had been stuck in a dead-end job, hopelessly depressed and being paid far less than the recognized legal minimum. I began to mull over the changes of the past few weeks, childishly dismissing as coincidence my peace pact with God, and the sudden change in my fortunes.

Nine months later the novelty had begun to wear off, although within this relatively short space of time I had already taken my first tentative steps into the world of relationships and sex. The spiritual side of my life had been cut down to an absolute minimum. Why should I bother, I thought, when I'm having so much fun in this new adult world, full of adventure? Besides I have the rest of my life in front of me.

Even the previously strained relationship with my mother seemed to improve, due mainly to the fact that I was spending much more time out and about with my friends. During one of my rare evenings spent at home watching television, an advertisement appeared for the Royal Air Force. Among the opportunities offered I couldn't help noticing the women, who looked really sexy in their neat blue uniforms. The advertisement faded with the words 'Train For A Trade'. Suddenly there it was again, that strange feeling of *déjà vu*. I made a note of the telephone number on the screen and three days later the information booklet arrived. I knew instinctively that this life was for me. This was exactly what I had been waiting for. I read carefully through the list of trades and what each entailed, until making up my mind to enlist as an electrician working on the aircraft. This would also enhance my future prospects in civilian life, I thought, already planning years ahead.

I filled in the application form, as neatly as possible, until I reached the last line: 'If under eighteen years of age, you must obtain the signature of a parent or guardian'. Following a short exchange with my mother, over the pros and cons of the matter, I was on my way to the letter box, dreaming once again of pulling on a uniform.

One week later I received the reply, inviting me to attend the recruitment office for a preliminary test and interview.

'You'd better iron a shirt and polish your shoes,' said my mother, at last seeming to respect my wishes.

The morning of my interview I awoke full of nervous excitement and began to polish my already gleaming shoes.

'Good luck!' called my mother, as I walked briskly towards the bus stop. I had already studied a map of the city centre and copied the easiest route down on a slip of paper. Safety first, I thought, not wishing to be late on my first encounter with the Royal Air Force.

Swing doors perfectly negotiated, I sat down in the packed waiting room. For some strange reason, I had expected to be the only person there.

'Next,' bellowed the desk sergeant.

'Heald, sir, Martin Heald,' I mumbled, embarrassed at the formality of the occasion. After the usual red-tape introductions and form filling, it was time for a medical.

'You'll pass,' said the medical orderly. 'Go back to the waiting room and wait for your name to be called out.'

After what felt like several hours, a sergeant checked and double-checked his list of names against the people present. We followed him into the examination room and took our places, ready for the test.

'OK, you lot, listen up, you have 30 minutes to complete the test. No talking or cheating, just do your best and good luck. You may begin.'

The 30 minutes were nearly up as I completed the last question. I didn't have a clue how I'd done, although the questions seemed relatively easy.

'OK, you will receive written notification regarding your test results, within two weeks.'

The sergeant, mellowed by this time, stood at the door shaking everyone's hand as we left, wishing us well for the future.

The next two weeks were torture. I hadn't given a moment's thought to the fact that I might actually fail the entrance test, until the sergeant had mentioned that if we were to fail it we would have to wait for a period of six months before being allowed to re-apply. Six whole months, I thought, deciding to banish any thought of failure from my mind.

*   *   *

'The postman's been,' said my mother, which meant that there was a letter for me! I nervously ripped open the envelope, thinking to myself, it's now or never.

'Dear Sir . . . Congratulations on your test results, you are invited for an intake interview on . . .' I couldn't believe my luck and threw the letter in the air, shouting in triumph.

'Well?' prompted my mother.

'Read it for yourself,' I said, as I ran up the stairs to get ready for work, already planning a celebratory drink for the evening.

On the day of my second interview I arrived full of expectation, ten minutes early at the recruitment office.

'Blimey, you're keen,' said the sergeant, fumbling in his uniform pocket for the keys to the building. After a quick chat and a cup of tea, the sergeant wished me good luck as he knocked on the officer's door.

'Enter,' shouted a rather upper-class voice.

'Martin Heald to see you, sir,' said the sergeant, after smartly saluting the portly officer.

'Have a seat, Heald, this won't take very long. Your test results were excellent, but there is one small problem.'

My heart sank.

'It's like this, you see,' began the officer. 'You wanted to join as an electrician, but the current waiting list is twelve months. What do you think, Heald, could you wait for another twelve months?' he asked, although he must have known by the look on my face, what the answer would be. 'Ah, I didn't think so, but there's no need to despair, I've got the very trade for you, if you're interested.'

'Yes, sir, I'm very interested. What sort of trade is it?'

'Well, I can't tell you too much, as it's covered by the Official Secrets Act. The only thing I can tell you is that it's an extremely challenging and exciting job, involving the use of computers, state of the art electronic aids and Morse code.'

I sat speechless. There it was again, Morse code.

'You don't have to give me an answer today.'

'Yes sir, I would like to be considered for the trade.'

'Good decision. You will be hearing from us shortly about a possible date for an aptitude test.' He shook my hand. 'Don't worry. Everything is taken care of by the Air Force, train fares, food and lodging.'

Morse code, I thought to myself on the way home, surely nobody uses such an outdated mode of communication nowadays.

Still, 'coincidence' had rescued me just in time I thought, the next day at work, after listening to the boss's son outlining his plans for the future of the company. They seemed to amount to the usual violation of the workers' hard-won rights. Longer working hours for the same pay, more discipline, including the wearing of a newly designed company uniform. Just another university graduate, with a head full of theory, combined with an insatiable ego. I consoled myself with thoughts of the forthcoming tests and interview, which I hoped would result in an offer to join the Royal Air Force, and give me my ticket out of there.

That was quick, I thought, carefully opening the familiar Air Force blue letter, which contained full travel instructions and my train tickets.

One week of sleepless nights later my date with destiny finally arrived. Waving goodbye to my mother I boarded the already delayed train to Leicester. I hoped that the agreed RAF transport would wait for the delayed train. Two hours later I arrived and there, sure enough, was the driver. After a brief introduction he threw my overnight bag on to the back seat of the RAF car.

Two hours on, the formalities had been completed and I flopped down on to the old-fashioned bed. My mind was totally focused on tomorrow's vitally important test. A final check – suit, shirt and tie neatly pressed, shoes polished, alarm clock set. Well, this was it, I thought, drifting off into unconsciousness.

Best night's sleep I'd had in years, I thought, sipping the cup of tea in the examination room. I had barely finished it when the sergeant entered the room.

'I will keep it short but sweet,' he began. 'In a moment, I will give you the test paper. All you have to do is listen to each set of Morse code characters in the headphones provided and mark off in the given squares whether you think that the letter is the same or different. Any questions?'

'No, I think that's clear enough,' I replied.

'OK, let's begin.'

Fifteen minutes later the test was complete.

'Well, what do you think?' asked the sergeant.

'I haven't got a clue,' I answered honestly.

'Any more questions?'

'Yes, how long will I have to wait for the results?'

'You should hear something by the end of next week.' The words still echoed inside my mind as the train approached Manchester Piccadilly station – my home town, I thought proudly.

'Fancy staying off work for a cold,' my workmates teased. If only I could tell them, I thought.

The end of the following week was fast approaching, sending me into a state of complete panic until finally, on the Thursday morning, my letter arrived. I hurriedly opened it. I could scarcely believe my eyes, there it was, that magical word, 'Congratulations'. I shouted so loud with joy that my mother, who was still in bed, came rushing to the top of the stairs.

'What's the matter?'

'I've been accepted. I have to go for a final intake interview in Manchester next week,' I told her excitedly.

'Well done, I knew you'd do it,' she replied, her voice shaking with emotion.

My workmates couldn't believe it.

'You're actually joining the RAF?' they repeated, for most of the following day, interspersed between nightmare stories about bullying and 'Once you've signed on the dotted line, that's it!' Were they speaking with more than a hint of jealousy, as they confronted their own bleak futures, stuck in a factory for the rest of their working lives?

My weekend was spent touring the local bars, celebrating my success with well-wishing friends, feeling rather ill on more than one occasion, until the day of my final interview arrived. This time I had absolutely no reason to feel nervous. I had made it, I thought, sitting in the familiar interview room, waiting for the officer.

'Congratulations,' he said reaching over the desk to shake my hand. 'Very impressive, your exam results, but don't let them go to your head,' he added sternly.

'What do you mean, sir?'

'Well, you are the first person in the history of the aptitude tests to achieve a score of one hundred per cent.'

My face flushed with embarrassment.

'Have you learnt Morse code before?'

'No sir, never.'

'Well, never mind, you are one of us now,' he said, as he handed me one of the many forms requiring my signature. 'OK, this envelope contains all the important information, day, date, time, train and camp, plus, should you decide to change your mind, a get-out-of-jail-free card,' he joked.

I was still on cloud nine, as I made myself a congratulatory cup of tea at home whilst trying to read the contents of the official-looking brown envelope.

Date of entrance, 15 April 1980. I couldn't believe my eyes, what a 'coincidence', the day after my late father's birthday and just two days after my own eighteenth birthday, my coming of age.

Suitcase neatly packed downstairs, I lay on my bed, reading my spiritual diary with the knowledge that, for now at least, my spiritual education would have to be put on a temporary hold; knowing also full well that the strange 'coincidences' would, sometime in the future, lead me once again towards that seemingly unavoidable spiritual path.

Six weeks of blood, sweat and tears later, the passing-out parade had finally arrived. One of the proudest moments of my life, I thought to myself, remembering how many people had dropped out or failed during the basic training.

The parade itself lasted an hour, although it felt more like ten minutes. Before I knew it, there I was, boarding the RAF coach which would be taking me to my new base, ready to commence the trade training.

The trade training itself was a more than welcome relief following those weeks of hell, reminding me immediately of my schooldays, although this time with a few important exceptions. The RAF tutor had a fantastic sense of humour and also treated everybody as an individual, which also created a friendly rivalry that lasted throughout the training.

My remarkable affiliation with Morse code continued. At the end of every week, the class would be tested on taking down Morse code at speed, the final target speed being 25 words per minute. My main rival and I passed the test on the same day, weeks ahead of the rest of the class. Morse code seemed to be second nature to me, it sounded so familiar. The nearest comparison I could think of was of somebody who had once learnt to type returning to type a letter after a 20-year gap, beginning somewhat rustily but soon being able to type as fast as ever.

Our camp had been chosen to host one of those fantastic air displays and, with the weekend fast approaching, the atmosphere began to reach fever pitch. Volunteers were being sought throughout the various trade classes; this meant giving up a free weekend to work, either on the car park or on one of the many stalls.

'Not one volunteer?' asked our class tutor.

Before I'd even thought about the consequences, I'd volunteered, much to the relief of the rest of the class. I had only seen one air show before, and that from the comfort of an armchair.

'Yes.' I convinced myself that I was looking forward to the event, in spite of giving up my free weekend.

I was allocated car park duty, which on the day didn't seem too bad, as it was a gloriously sunny day. The traffic soon began to build up and within two hours the car park was full to capacity, signalling in effect the end of my day's duty. I raced back to barracks and changed quickly into civilian clothes, ready to enjoy the afternoon's events. The show began with modern jet fighters, followed swiftly by an unannounced appearance of the Red Arrows formation flying team. I couldn't help but admire the pilots' skill. One of the manoeuvres involved two of the aircraft flying towards each other at breathtaking speed, then breaking off in different directions at the very last moment. I was just about to leave, not really wishing to listen to the closing speech, when the distant sound of approaching aircraft rooted me to the spot. Two minutes later, three aircraft flew directly above the already dispersing crowd – a Lancaster bomber, flanked on either side by Spitfires. The magnificence of the Lancaster, combined with the almost deafening roar of its engines, seemed to transport me back in time, but to a time that I couldn't possibly have been a part of. I must have puzzled for hours, trying to come up with a logical explanation for my feelings and the emotions that followed. I didn't actually cry, despite the lump in my throat. Whilst I did not recognize the significance of this event at the time, I can see now that 'coincidence' had struck again, in an attempt to increase my spiritual awareness.

*　*　*

The next three years flew by. What have I accomplished? I asked myself. All that remained was a hazy recollection of drinking sessions, parties and work.

It was during one of the cheese and wine parties that I started to feel a strange dizziness come over me. Although I'd drunk quite a few too many glasses of wine, I knew that this unearthly feeling had nothing to do with being intoxicated. I made some sort of excuse to the rest of the party and half walked, half staggered back to my room. After closing the door behind me I swilled my face with cold water and stared into the mirror. My heart missed a couple of beats as I gazed at the stranger's face looking back at me. His facial features seemed familiar but they certainly bore no resemblance to mine. I was just about to rub my eyes when the stranger's face disappeared, to be replaced by my own blood-drained and rather haggard-looking reflection.

'Must be drunk,' I muttered to myself as I lay down on the bed and switched off the bedside lamp, hoping that the room wouldn't decide to show me its own special version of a spinning top!

I'd been on my bed for about ten minutes, or so I thought, when a distinct sound of buzzing began to disturb me. Where's it coming from? I thought, opening my eyes and peering around the darkened room. The noise seemed to be emanating from underneath my bed and as I turned my head around slowly to have a look, I got the shock of my life. There, on the bed, approximately three feet below me, lay my fully clothed body, snoring away as if there were no tomorrow. After the initial shock had subsided I began to worry about how I could get back into my slumbering body, when a sudden jolt pushed me into the corridor, clean through the solid concrete wall. It was then that I realized that I wasn't completely alone – something or somebody stood directly behind me. I tried my utmost to turn around to face this person to demand an explanation.

'Please remain calm, Martin. I am one of your spiritual guides,' began the hauntingly familiar voice. 'I have been sent to accompany you on this journey. If you have any questions, please wait until the end of the journey. You have absolutely nothing to fear; just stay calm and observe.'

I'd barely had time to take in the words when the corridor disappeared, to be replaced by an extremely powerful and dazzlingly bright light. After a few moments I could see a large house directly in front of me, surrounded by the most breathtaking scenery I had ever seen. I began to make my way slowly towards the house, watching in amazement as the green grass beneath me began to change colour. I must have counted at least sixteen different hues of green before I reached the open doorway. As I crossed the threshold a sudden jolt of emotion coursed through me as a brief moment of recognition suffused my very being. That four-poster bed – I could have sworn that I'd seen it somewhere before. Everything about the house looked so familiar, the decor, the style, so simple yet stunningly effective. I stared out of one of the windows and noticed a stream of clear blue and green water, which meandered down the hillside, until finally joining a torrent of waterfalls which fed a river of azure blue stretching into the distance as far as the eye could see.

This must be a dream, I thought to myself, deciding to walk down to the river for a swim, reasoning to myself that if I was dreaming, the sudden temperature change might perhaps bring me back to my slumbering body, wherever it was.

That wasn't there before, I thought, looking at the envelope on top of the ornamental fireplace. Curiosity got the better of me as I carefully opened the blank envelope and, feeling rather guilty, began to read its neatly written contents.

> My darling Richard, or Martin as you are now called, by the time you read this you will probably wonder what is going on, and maybe you will not fully understand the contents, but I am your soulmate Jennifer and this is our home. You probably won't be able to remember this, but we have spent countless lifetimes together, in various incarnations. At this present moment, in your earthly existence, you have strayed away from your chosen path and are wasting your opportunities. You must begin to listen to your inner self, otherwise it may be too late and we will not meet up as planned, with all the consequences which could follow.
>
> I know that this must seem ridiculous, being lectured to by a stranger but I can only ask you to trust my words. Please return to your spiritual destiny before it's too late.
>
> Hope to meet you soon, love forever . . . Jen

I placed the letter back where I'd found it, and dumbfoundedly made my way out of the house and towards the river, wondering if the letter was meant for me, or the mysteriously named 'Richard'.

I sat on the riverbank gazing deeply into the fast-flowing river, thinking about my life so far, until the realization soon began to dawn. All my life I'd been drawn to the spiritual dimension, and yet here I was for the first time in my life completely cut off from even the slightest hint of anything spiritual. The only spirits I had in mind were of the alcoholic variety. I began to wonder when I'd last gone more than a few days without a drink, until the terrifying truth hit me – I was slowly but surely becoming dependent upon alcohol. My spiritual studies had dwindled away into a seemingly endless bout of boozy oblivion.

I sat there in total despair, wondering how on earth I'd let myself sink so low, when I noticed the distinct figure of a fair-haired woman approaching me. This must be an angel, I thought, staring at the smiling emerald-green eyes, that were, I felt, peering into my very soul.

'My name's Juliette and, yes, Martin, before you ask, we have met before.'

I stood up to shake Juliette's outstretched hand and was immediately engulfed by such a feeling of warmth, love and tranquillity that I thought I would faint.

'Listen Martin, I know you must be confused at the moment, but just try to relax and enjoy this experience, because you will have to return to your body quite soon.'

I'd hardly had time to collect my thoughts when the scenery suddenly changed and I found myself sitting on a warm, dew-dappled grass mat. A tremendous surge of love and happiness welled up inside me, as I tried to take in this wonderful Garden of Eden. I could see small groups of people deep in conversation, radiating a love and inner happiness that one could only ever dream of on Earth. Young, angelic-looking children were playing happily amongst themselves, and picking all manners of strangely coloured exotic fruits from the branches of pastel-coloured trees, placing them in small baskets, woven out of fine silky webbing.

'Do you remember this place?' asked Juliette.

'I don't think so,' I replied, hesitantly. 'I'm sure that if I'd been here before I would have remembered.'

'This is just a small reminder of what awaits you when you return here next time. You may stay here for a while until David comes to pick you up.'

I said goodbye to Juliette and lay down in the long warm

grass, after watching her disappear into the distance. I couldn't remember falling asleep but the next instant I could hear the familiar voice of my first guide calling out my name. My whole being seemed to be vibrating as I stared at the white-robed, silvery-bearded figure standing in front of me.

'You haven't got much more time now, Martin. Just do as I ask and everything will be all right.'

Following his instructions, I sat down on an extremely soft and comfortable floor in a triangular-shaped room, wondering what had happened to the Garden of Eden. A sudden change in the atmosphere made me aware that something was going on above my head. As I looked up I saw what seemed to me like the world's largest and purest diamond, moving slowly downwards, its point directly over the middle of my head. Before I'd had a chance to think, a strong charge of light energy coursed through me. I sat there, completely amazed, watching a rapid but clear review of my life up until that present moment. Apparently I had reached an important stage of development in my life, and some of the decisions I would be making shortly would have a drastic effect on my own and other people's lives.

I was shown, in detail, the seemingly endless possibilities open to me and their probable consequences. The sequence ended as suddenly as it had begun and I found myself standing once again, in front of this nameless guide.

'I know I promised you that you could ask some questions, Martin, but unfortunately we have run out of time.'

I was just about to say something when the guide reached over and covered my eyes with a cotton cloth.

I found myself on my bed, awake, and tried to switch my bedside lamp on. I couldn't move a muscle, my whole body seemed to be paralysed. I lay staring at the ceiling in frustration, knowing full well that the experience couldn't possibly have been 'only' a dream, and hoped desperately that I would be able to recall my experience in the cold and sober light of day. As it was, by the following day the 'dream' had been all but forgotten, at least for a time.

Several weeks later I was sitting in the mess hall enjoying a meal of steak and chips and looking forward to a night on the town with a small group of colleagues. Suddenly fragments of the strange 'dream' began to filter through into my consciousness, especially concerning my alcohol consumption. I decided to stay in for this one evening, if only to prove to myself that I could go without alcohol for once.

After making my excuses to my drinking buddies, I went back to my room and lay down on the bed, listening to a music cassette. There was a rap at the door and Gerry, my next-door neighbour, burst in, shaking me out of my reverie.

'What are you doing on your own, you hermit?' he said.

'I thought you were going out with the rest of the gang,' I replied, feeling a little annoyed at this sudden intrusion.

'Well, I changed my mind and was wondering if you fancied having a go on my Ouija board?'

Excitedly, I remembered my childhood experiences with the Ouija board.

'Get it set up and I will be with you in five minutes,' I said, full of anticipation.

Seated at the table with Gerry, I quickly assumed command and ten minutes later we'd made our first contact, although the messages didn't seem to make the slightest bit of sense. Gerry soon began to lose interest and started to mock the contact.

'Don't do that,' I scolded, as by now the room temperature had begun to drop menacingly.

'Is that the best you can do?' taunted Gerry, who obviously hadn't sensed the sudden change in atmosphere. I left him alone in the room while I visited the toilet, and was in the process of washing my hands, when I heard a terrifying scream, followed swiftly by the sound of footsteps. Gerry burst into the toilet area, his face white.

'What's up with you?' I asked jokingly. 'Seen a ghost?'

'The table,' Gerry repeated three times.

I looked into his genuinely frightened eyes, and realized something serious had happened. Apparently, after I'd left the room to visit the toilet, the heavy table that we'd been using had levitated to approximately two feet from the ground and come crashing down with a bump, sending the Ouija board flying through the air.

'Well, I must admit, you're a hell of a good actor, Gerry.'

'It's the truth!' he protested, as we walked back to the room. The table certainly had moved from its original position and the board and pointer were on the floor, on the opposite side of the room.

'Are you going to help me to tidy the room up tomorrow?' asked Gerry, rather sheepishly, I thought.

'Give me a shout in the morning, then.'

The following day, both Gerry and I were on the evening shift, and as Gerry was vacating the large 12-man room, to move into a single room on his own, I'd offered to help him to clean it. I'd just arrived back in my room after breakfast, when Gerry walked in.

'Feeling fit, Martin?'

Following a brief discussion about the events of the previous evening Gerry went off to find the communal block sweeping brush. After lying lazily sprawled across my bed for 20 minutes, wondering where on earth Gerry had got to, I decided to make a start on the task in hand. I walked out into the corridor armed with a couple of dusters and polish, and was just walking towards Gerry's room when the door began to knock rhythmically. Gerry must have started without me, I thought, listening to what I was sure was the sound of a sweeping brush banging into the door.

'I thought you were going to give me a shout,' I said sarcastically, as I neared the frosted-glass window, set in the middle of the door.

The knocking increased in intensity to an almost impossible rate. The hairs on the back of my neck stood up in fright, as the realization hit me that there was nobody in Gerry's room. I took a few paces back and watched in fascinated horror as the door nearly jumped off its hinges.

This is impossible, I thought, rooted to the spot, an unwilling observer. The door itself, including the frosted glass, had gone through a series of twists, bends and turns, without shattering the glass or splintering the wood. I managed to regain control of my senses, turned swiftly and started to run down the corridor. Just before I'd made it to the other door the deafening noise had suddenly stopped, as Gerry opened the door armed with a sweeping brush and cleaning materials.

'Is there anybody else supposed to be helping us?'

'No, why do you ask?'

I related the sequence of events to Gerry, as we searched the room.

'Well, there's nobody in here. You must have been imagining things,' joked Gerry.

We cleaned the room in double-quick time, as it was getting

late. Gerry locked the door behind us, and we quickly changed into our uniforms ready for the evening shift, which proved as boring and uneventful as usual.

At the end of the shift, Gerry and I made our way via the guardroom to the mess hall, for a welcome hot supper before retiring to bed.

'They're going to inspect that room tomorrow,' said Gerry, before disappearing towards his new one-man room. It should pass the inspection, no problem, I thought, reaching over to switch off my bedside lamp.

I had just reached that borderline state between consciousness and unconsciousness when a shattering noise jolted me awake. I lay there in the semi-darkness wondering where the noise had come from and remembered the strange events from the morning. I dismissed the distressing thought and redoubled my efforts to fall asleep. Within seconds, it sounded as though hell had been let loose in Gerry's former room, which unfortunately was opposite mine. I jumped out of bed and switched on the light. I stood stock still, listening to what sounded like wardrobes and bedside lockers being thrown around the room, accompanied by a hammering noise on my own bedroom wall.

Why hasn't anybody else in the block heard all the bedlam? I wondered, as the din stopped. I sat down on the bed and tremblingly lit a cigarette, in a vain effort to get things into perspective. I'd nearly finished my cigarette when I heard a blood-curdling scream, followed swiftly by the distinct sound of heavy footsteps in the other room. I mentally followed the footsteps, until they had reached the door. You won't get through that I thought bravely, remembering that Gerry had locked the door and handed the keys in to the guardroom staff.

The hairs on my neck stood up as I heard the door opening. That's impossible, I thought, listening in terror as the footsteps stopped outside my door momentarily, before continuing on down the corridor and finally passing out of earshot, to my intense relief.

By this time, I'd decided to vacate my room and go and sleep on Gerry's floor. The trouble was, that I would have to negotiate the corridor first.

Ah well, it's now or never, I thought, trying to open my door as quietly as possible. I stepped out into the corridor, my heart thumping. I'd taken a first few steps when a morbid curiosity came over me. I had to see if I'd been dreaming, or whether these events had really taken place.

I turned around slowly and sure enough the door itself was ajar, confirming my worst fears. I was still shaking as I related the terrifying events to a half-conscious Gerry.

The ear-piercing sound of Gerry's bedside alarm clock woke me up the next morning. I thanked him for the use of his floor and walked stiffly towards my own room. To my sheer amazement, the door to the room was now shut, I plucked up enough courage to try the handle, It was securely locked. Shortly afterwards, the entire block was condemned and we all moved to a newly refurbished block, much to my relief.

Another lesson learnt the hard way, I thought, deciding never to touch an Ouija board again. I'd heard all of the negative stories surrounding the Ouija board but, due to my own childhood experiences, had never believed them, until now!

It was around the time of this incident that I began to feel something was missing from my life. My intuition had begun to plant seeds of doubt and confusion in my mind and following a seemingly endless battle between intuition and logic, I finally decided to leave the RAF. This decision was made much easier by the fact that by then I had met and fallen in love with my future wife, who lived in my home city of Manchester.

I handed in my resignation in April that year, much to the surprise of my friends and less than three weeks later I received notification of my last day in the RAF, 26 November 1983.

Most of the remaining few months I spent wondering about my drastic decision. What on earth was I going to do? I didn't even have a job to go to. The only security I had was the promise of a roof over my head from my future mother-in-law; this would at least give my girlfriend and me a chance to live together, before we made our final commitment to each other.

My last day in the Royal Air Force was filled with a host of conflicting emotions. On the one hand, I was gaining freedom, both spiritual and physical; on the other hand I was losing a number of precious relationships, built up during the last three years.

Sadness soon changed to happiness, though, as I recognized

my girlfriend's smiling face amongst the crowd of people around the station platform. Following an emotional and passionate welcome, we climbed into her mother's car for the short journey to my new home.

FOUR

Following a short settling-in period, the need to earn a living wage became painfully obvious. My girlfriend and I yearned for the privacy of our own home. I wrote letter after letter, without success. I was beginning to have doubts about my decision to leave the security of the Air Force until, during a particularly deep bout of depression, I received the flash of inspiration I had been waiting for.

I set out at once to visit my mother, who had re-married, taking with me a large bag to collect my library of spiritual books, which were still hidden in my former sanctuary.

One particular book about meditation seemed to stand out from the rest, although I couldn't fathom out why. Could this be the same book that I had bought five years previously and almost thrown away, unable to find anything to interest me amongst all the complicated Tibetan language, not to mention the highly disciplined exercises? Now it took me less than a day, to read the book from cover to cover and choose the exercise that seemed to meet my needs.

It told you to meditate three times a day, using the powerful visualization method, combined with a special breathing exercise which would, according to the instructions, enable one to filter the exact frequencies of light energy necessary for this particular meditation.

The first two days of meditation proved to be the most difficult, especially the breathing exercise which involved closing the right nostril and breathing in to a count of four through the left nostril. Instead of exhaling which of course comes naturally, one must hold the breath for 16 seconds, and then exhale to the count of eight through the right nostril; the whole process was then repeated, only this time beginning with the closure of the left nostril.

The visualization seemed to be a lot simpler, due mainly to the fact that I could employ my fantasy. All you had to do was to strongly visualize a pulsating golden orb of energy above your head, which then passed gradually down your entire body, while simultaneously holding a clear picture of the desired result, which in my case of course was a job with a reasonable wage.

Two weeks later I started my new job as a postman. I was so relieved and excited that I'd almost forgotten the meditations I'd carried out the week before. Another 'coincidence' I thought, not really caring how I'd managed to get the job.

My Post Office career started promisingly enough, when I broke the sorting office record for the number of letters sorted per minute, which had stood for a number of years. However, the extremely early morning starts soon began to play havoc with my biological body clock. I was turning, slowly but surely, into a short-tempered exhausted zombie, which in turn brought about a strain in my relationship with both my girlfriend, and her patient family.

Following almost a year of frustration working for the Post Office, I'd nearly reached the end of the line, when my girlfriend offered to put in a good word for me at the factory where she worked. Less than two weeks later, after a short interview with my new employer, I'd said goodbye to the Post Office and started my new job, as a machine operator in the same building as my girlfriend. As fate would have it, I ended up working twice as hard, although I was also earning more than three times the amount I'd earned as a postman.

My girlfriend and I opened a joint savings account, having already decided to buy our own house, hopefully in the near future. This newly found security had at last given us the opportunity to set a date for our wedding, September 1984. Following the wedding and honeymoon, we moved into our new house. At last, I thought, alone with my new wife, plus the chance to resume my badly neglected spiritual studies.

I had already tried to speak to my wife about the strange events in my life and my spiritual practices. Judging by her indifferent reactions, I decided to keep this side of my life to myself, not wishing to rock the boat at such an early stage of our marriage.

My experiments began once again in earnest, since I had wasted, in my opinion some three years of my life, in the RAF. The new sense of freedom was almost intoxicating. No need to hide any of my books or paraphernalia, nobody to ask awkward questions. I was on cloud nine, both physically and spiritually.

Strange coincidences once again became a part of my life, just as they had been before I had joined the RAF, only this time. I had begun to notice a direct correlation between the various situations I had fantasized during a meditation and the actual material events that were occurring around me.

My wife and I had been invited to an engagement party, but as the evening of the party approached I found that I had lost my initial enthusiasm. I just couldn't seem to be able to cope with parties any more. All those people crammed into a small building, doing their utmost to hide their emotions, thoughts and feelings. Now, all of a sudden, I could sense, hear and almost taste every single cooped-up emotion. It seemed to me that the more people drank, the more emotions would escape and eventually find their way towards, and invade, my own emotional field, which more often than not would leave me feeling depressed, without any logical reason. Although I had once read a book, in the safety of my attic sanctuary in Manchester, which touched on the subject of protecting one's own energy field, I had brushed aside the subject with a mixture of arrogance and youthful exuberance; now I wasn't so sure. After a short and noisy quarrel with my wife, I decided against my better judgement to go with her to the party. As we began the short walk to where the party was being held, I caught a glimpse of the building in my mind's eye, completely plunged into darkness. That's weird, I thought, beginning to tease my wife.

'Just think, there could be a power cut; yes, that's a good idea, perhaps if I concentrated hard enough, it would happen.'

'Don't say that,' said my wife, not for a moment taking me seriously.

As we arrived outside the entrance to the building, a small disgruntled group was standing outside, talking among themselves in obvious annoyance.

'What's going on?' asked my wife.

'The party has been cancelled. A workman digging up a nearby road has cut through the electricity cable!'

Needless to say, the walk back home took place in stony silence.

A few months had passed by since the unfortunate 'coincidence' and I was beginning to feel a little frustrated. Yes, I had the privacy I had yearned for and I seemed to be making exceptional progress, but I had no one to share my enthusiasm with, nobody I could talk to about spiritual matters. I read with envy the stories of small groups who were busy studying and practising the various spiritual aspects of life. I hoped that one day I would be lucky enough to be able to join such a group, although the chances were very limited, due to the strict code of secrecy amongst their members.

In an attempt to console myself, I decided to treat myself to a new book from a specialist bookshop in Manchester. I'd been browsing for almost an hour, when a small brightly coloured leaflet caught my eye, advertising incense imported from all over the world. I hadn't used incense for a long time and decided to take the leaflet home, where I could read it at leisure. The prices advertised seemed to be quite reasonable so I carefully filled in the order form and wrote the company's address on an envelope. Strangely enough, it was a PO box number in London, of all places. I wondered how the leaflet had managed to end up in a Manchester bookstore.

Two weeks later I received a written reply:

Dear Martin,
Thank you for your enquiry regarding our range of incenses. Regretfully we have been forced to cease trading, due to legal reasons. We are, however, continuing with our group study, meeting once or twice in the month. We are always on the look out for suitable individuals to join our small but dedicated group. You are hereby invited to attend our next meeting, without any obligation. Should you decide to attend, I would be delighted to hear from you on the above telephone number.

I could scarcely believe my luck – this was exactly what I had hoped for. Coincidence had once again presented me with a window of opportunity. After speaking to the woman on the telephone, the 'coincidence' seemed all the more extraordinary. Apparently, the mail order leaflets had been taken out of circulation 18 months previously and, last but not least, the meetings were held in Manchester, less than 20 minutes away by train.

I arrived ten minutes late for my first meeting, as the train had been delayed. The leader introduced me to the other members of the group, people from all walks of life, a magistrate, a teacher, university graduates, plus a whole host of different occupations. After my somewhat nervous introduction, the leader of the group began to explain its main objectives.

'Our group was formed three years ago, mainly out of concern for our planet, which is being systematically poisoned by nuclear testing, the destruction and desecration of vitally important rain forests and the production of chemicals, which will eventually poison the earth's atmosphere. The warning signs have already begun to appear, in the shape of crop circles which, after careful scientific research, have proved to be of extra-terrestrial origin.'

The leader went on to describe various rituals and meditations, all designed to increase our spiritual consciousness, which in turn would lead to a general rise of spiritual consciousness around the world, due to the domino effect of this universal law of nature.

I was completely overawed, listening intently to the information I was being given. Somewhere deep down inside of me I knew that the information contained more than a hint of truth. During the short interval, burning with curiosity, I asked the leader about the so-called 'crop circles'. She reached a book from an over-filled bookcase, which she handed to me.

'Here you are, this should satisfy your curiosity.'

I opened the book and after studying the contents quickly turned over the pages to look at the aerial photographs. An inexplicable feeling of *déjà vu* came over me. I recognized the perfectly formed geometric figures but couldn't for the life of me think where I'd seen them before. I certainly hadn't read about them and couldn't recall ever seeing them on the television, or could I?

The evening was completed by way of a group meditation, using a combination of mantras and visualization designed, according to the leader, to cleanse and strengthen our energy fields. The effects were amazing. The whole group, including myself, sitting in a circle hands joined, eyes closed, began simultaneously to chant the given mantra, in between whiffs of the sweet cloying incense. After a few minutes of chanting, I began to lose the awareness of my body and started on a swift ascent, until coming to an abrupt halt, far above the earth, which appeared to be the size of a football. The next moment, there I was, back once more in my still chanting body. The experience itself must have lasted seconds, but would I felt stay with me forever.

The words of the leader were still fresh in my mind on the homeward journey.

'Remember Martin, it's no coincidence that you've been sent here; it's karma, a part of your spiritual education.'

I was still on cloud nine and looking forward to the next meeting, wondering if such experiences would be repeated during future meditational sessions.

The next few meetings of the group proved to me beyond any shadow of a doubt that our paths had been intended to cross. The spiritual leader had telephoned each of the group members and asked if we would bring a photograph of any sick relatives or friends to the following meeting, adding that we would be doing a powerful healing ritual. I didn't know anybody within my family or circle of friends who was ill, or in any way disabled, although on the night of the meeting it didn't seem to matter as the rest of the group emptied their heaps of photographs on the table.

The leader explained the ritual.

'We will be using an extremely powerful mantra. The breathing must be controlled and concentrated, beginning with a deep breath in, to the count of seven seconds, holding this breath in for seven seconds and exhaling for exactly seven seconds. Does everyone understand?'

Ten minutes later, we'd all assembled in the ritual chamber and, as instructed, formed a near-perfect circle around the photographs, which had been neatly placed on the carpeted floor. The incense-filled room could have been situated on the other side of the universe as far as I was concerned. The tense situation had created an other worldly atmosphere, where time and space, in the normal sense of the word, had ceased to exist.

The eerie sound of the ritual bell resonated around the darkened room, sending an instant electrical charge through the gathering. I closed my eyes and in accordance with our instructions began to breathe in deeply, until the sound of the bell indicated that seven seconds had passed. Following seven minutes of the breathing exercise, I'd just started to adjust to the dizziness and disorientation when the mantra began. The whole room seemed to vibrate with a tingling energy, which slowly pulsated through my body, beginning with my feet, until finally reaching my extremely overactive and curious brain. I couldn't hold back any longer and decided to open my eyes to see what was going on. This is unbelievable, I thought to myself, staring at the spectral play unfolding before me.

The spiritual leader was seated in a cross-legged position in our chanting midst and seemed to be in some sort of deep trance state. I watched in awe as what appeared to be hundreds upon hundreds of spirits were arriving one after the other and disappearing into the motionless body of our leader. After approximately 20 seconds the stream of spirits ceased, followed immediately by an almost blinding blue and white light, which emanated from the middle of the leader's forehead and concentrated itself into a perfect arc, which passed directly through the photographs. I closed my eyes quickly, realizing that I'd probably been witness to something that no other human being had ever seen.

The ritual bell brought an abrupt end to an emotionally charged session and following an informal conversation we each went our separate ways, with a promise to telephone the leader, should any of the patients' conditions change.

The train journey home was over in a flash, as I tried to make sense of the evening's startling events and hoped that the leader hadn't seen me observing what to me was the 'impossible'.

Several weeks later, I had almost forgotten the amazing healing ritual, although my own life had completely changed. I felt on top of the world. No situation, no matter how desperate it seemed, could get me down. My consciousness had been raised to such an extent that I could rise above the usual ups and downs of life in this hectic and seemingly unfair western society and for the first time in my life I felt that my eventual destiny lay in my own hands.

The group's next few monthly gatherings were no less amazing, especially after listening to the unbelievable accounts from the individual members concerning the healing session. Apparently at least seven of the patients who were quite seriously ill, had made either a partial or complete recovery, much to the surprise of their sceptical specialists.

As we were coming to the closing meditational ceremony on my twelfth visit the leader congratulated me on my enthusiasm and continued support for the group, adding that my moment of enlightenment wouldn't be far off.

'You see, Martin, our group's work has to be carried out in relative secrecy, especially considering the nature of our tasks. With the current climate of negative media witch hunting, we would be better off not coming to the attention of the press; not that we have anything to hide, we just don't want to take the risk of being misunderstood and being branded as heretics. During your next visit you will be able to understand why we ask for this secrecy. Your next meeting will be your thirteenth, a number which is usually connected with bad luck but, as you will see, this number has had and will continue to have a great significance in your life.'

I spent the next few weeks in a state of great confusion, wondering if I was being conned by the group. The leader had mentioned something about an oracle and that mere words could not do the experience any justice. The leader's parting words were still tantalizing my mind: 'Everyone who joins the group and passes our tests, has earned the right to see the oracle.'

What tests? I wondered, absent-mindedly staring out of the train window into a darkened Manchester evening sky, on my way to the group's meeting place. As I entered the ritual chamber the air seemed to be filled with anticipation, and after the usual introductory chit-chat the leader ushered me into one of the smaller rooms where a steaming bath, full of strangely coloured and highly aromatic bath salts, awaited me.

'Now, before you are allowed to see the oracle, you must soak yourself in this herbal bath for exactly 30 minutes. I will give you a shout when we are ready,' announced the leader solemnly as she left the room.

What on earth have I let myself in for? I wondered, slowly lowering myself into the steaming hot bath. After 30 minutes had passed, I climbed out of the herbal bath, feeling strangely invigorated and refreshed. After quickly drying myself on one of the neatly arranged towels, I stepped into the one-piece orange-coloured toga, that had been provided especially for the ritual.

The leader knocked on the bathroom door and said that they were ready for me. I opened the door and followed her back towards the ritual chamber, feeling rather silly wearing such an outrageous garment. As we entered the chamber I noticed that the carpet had been rolled back to the other side of the room, revealing an open trap door with a set of narrow steps spiralling downward into the bowels of the earth.

I distinctly heard the sound of muffled voices as I followed the leader down the steps until we finally reached our destination. The room itself was completely circular, its walls and the ceiling were covered with mirrors, enhancing the strangeness of the whole situation. The rest of the group sat around in a circle quietly talking amongst themselves until our arrival.

'Let us begin,' said the leader, as two members moved to one side to make room for us. I watched in total fascination as she removed a black, silky-looking piece of material from the centre of the floor, to reveal what appeared to be a small well, filled with mercury.

'Light the candles and turn off the light.'

The room was immediately plunged into an eerie semi-darkness, punctuated by the almost continual flickering of the candles.

'I want you to relax completely, and stare into the oracle until I end the session.' This was clearly addressed to me. I tried my best to relax in these unnatural circumstances, and stared into the silver-coloured liquid as the whole group began to chant in a strange language. After a few minutes the liquid began to mist over, to be in turn replaced by what appeared to be some sort of cinema film. I watched in dumbfounded silence as the pictures unfolded. According to the film the earth would, in the not-too-distant future, undergo a series of complete and for some nations disastrous upheavals. I felt more than a little uncomfortable as the terrible scenes unfolded before me: earthquakes, volcanoes, tidal waves and a whole set of natural disasters. The years and approximate dates flew by along with the sad sight of the world powers arguing amongst themselves, trying in vain to place the blame on any power but their own.

The film continued, with the news that enlightened spiritual leaders and prophets would suddenly appear in all four corners of the globe and, working simultaneously, would take the earth into a new spiritual era.

My *déjà vu*-filled evening ended too soon. When I tried to ask the leader one of a thousand questions that I'd had, she brushed it aside, asking me to be patient and adding that I would understand the significance of the evening in the coming months and years.

The slow train journey home offered no solace, as I ran the evening's events through my mind over and over again.

Two years later the situation within the group had become intolerable, due to needless and seemingly endless arguments, and the leader's insatiable ego, a combination which spelt the end of my love affair with the group. This decision was made much easier by the birth of my daughter.

I continued my spiritual studies alone, making use of the extremely valuable knowledge and wisdom I had gained during my short period with the group and felt more than a little sadness and disappointment at having to leave what was in hindsight a very genuine and motivated set of people. Meanwhile, although I hadn't noticed it, I was beginning to neglect my wife and daughter.

FIVE

The strain of working 70 hours a week in a hot and dirty environment soon began to take its toll. I seemed to need every spare minute of my free time to sleep, but my wife seemed to be coping adequately, bringing up our daughter who had by this stage begun to walk. Petty arguments between my wife and me soon became a part of our life until, following my return from a fishing trip with a work colleague, my wife announced that she'd had enough of the situation and asked me to move out of our family home for a week, to give her time to think the situation over. The words hit me like a bombshell. I just couldn't believe what I'd heard. I'd been so self-centred that I'd failed to notice the obvious warning signs. Following a brief discussion I decided to stay at my mother's house for a week, to give my wife the space and time necessary to make whatever decision she deemed appropriate.

At the end of a tense week I telephoned my wife to hear the bad news that she wished for a separation. I was completely heartbroken. What on earth had I done to deserve such treatment? How could I cope without seeing my daughter?

My wife agreed to let me move back home until I could find somewhere else to live. I tried for two weeks to get her to change her mind, to no avail. By this time, I had a new job and found myself working even more unsociable hours, six nights a week in a local bakery. However, the financial rewards more than made up for any lack of social life and, besides, the need for any sort of social life had evaporated, due to my emotional situation.

Scanning the local newspapers, I soon managed to find a

suitable enough house to share and, having met the two residents, I decided to move in, after taking half of my worldly belongings to my mother's house.

My new housemates soon made me feel at home, the atmosphere was so different, so much more relaxed. Emily worked as a cleaner at a local factory and David was an office clerk. They both went out of their way to cheer me up as best they could, without being too overbearing, and the three of us soon struck up a fantastic relationship, while at the same time appreciating the others' needs for privacy, especially as there were no locks on the bedroom doors.

I was still working nights at the bakers and sleeping during the day, usually until around mid-afternoon, when Emily would wake me up with a cup of tea.

'Martin,' she began, 'I hope you don't shout at me, but last night when you were at work, I decided to clean your bedroom and stumbled across your collection of books and couldn't help but browse through a few of them!'

'Yes, get to the point,' I retorted, rather angry at this blatant intrusion on my privacy.

'Well, it's like this. I've had quite a problem in finding a partner and thought maybe you could organize something for me.'

"What on earth do you mean?' I asked, knowing full well which book she had read.

'I know you are different,' began Emily. 'David and I discussed the change in the atmosphere, since you arrived.'

In the end I agreed to try and help Emily, and decided to meditate every evening before I set off to work. This seemed to appease Emily until around two weeks later she began to pester me, refusing to listen to any logical reason why, despite my daily meditations, she still hadn't met anybody. Three days later she woke me up, excitedly exclaiming, 'It's happened, I've got a date this evening!' A man who worked at one of the local garages had offered to take her out for a drink. Emily thanked me profusely, leaving me in peace to drink my cup of tea.

At last, I thought to myself, 'coincidence' had once again rescued me, from what was fast becoming a potentially sticky situation.

A few months later, David departed for London, to live with his new girlfriend, leaving Emily and me alone in the house. By this time, though, Emily's new boyfriend seemed to be spending more and more time with her. I'd still not had a chance to introduce myself, due to the unsociable hours I was working, until one particularly noisy weekend I decided to interrupt their fun, to complain about the noise.

'Hello friend, pleased to meet you at last; Emily has told me so much about you.'

My initial anger subsided, as the stranger shook my hand and introduced himself. Emily left the room to make a cup of tea, giving Shaun and me a chance to get acquainted. It soon became apparent that Shaun had been drinking, his slurred speech at first hard to follow. After five awkward minutes, listening to Shaun's life story, I was just about to make my excuses, when he told me his birth date, 13th April.

'What a coincidence,' I interrupted. 'That's my birthday!' The conversation that followed seemed more akin to a science fiction film than reality. Apparently Shaun's father's birthday was the day after his, exactly the same as my father's; we had even named our daughters the same. We were both in an almost identical situation, apart from the fact that Shaun had turned to alcohol in a vain attempt to escape the emotions and the situation he had found himself in.

My introduction to Shaun made me realize just how lucky I was, despite having gone through a similar set of experiences and circumstances. I hadn't been drawn into that desperate world of alcoholism, relying mainly upon my spiritual convictions to see me eventually through this emotional hell of divorce.

A short time later, thanks to our landlord, Emily and I moved to a larger, more modern house and were told to expect new house-mates in a month or two. Luckily, the relationship between Emily and Shaun seemed to be blossoming, leaving me alone to continue my research. My meditations, I had noticed, were becoming deeper and lasting much longer than at any previous time, until, during one particularly deep session, I must have fallen asleep and began to dream vividly about a television report.

'The aircraft burst into flames halfway down the runway, following what eyewitnesses reported to be a dull explosion,' announced the newscaster. Pictures of the stricken aircraft were shown, followed by the number of casualties and dead. I woke in a cold sweat, wondering what on earth the dream could mean, especially as it had seemed so real. I finally put it down to an adult nightmare, until a week later.

'Hey Martin, have you seen today's news?' enquired Emily. 'Terrible, all those people involved.'

'What are you talking about?' I asked, a little bemused.

'The aircraft accident at the airport, haven't you heard about it?'

I decided to watch the evening news, wondering what the fuss was about. I sat in front of the television in stony silence, a cold sweat breaking out over my whole body. There it was, exactly as I had dreamed, the same aircraft, the same newscaster, right down to the eyewitness report.

'What's the matter, Martin? You've gone all white.'

I relayed my dream to Emily, expecting a response of disbelief. 'Nothing surprises me about you,' she replied nonchalantly, quickly leaving the room to answer the telephone, leaving me alone to ponder my first premonition.

The sound of the doorbell brought me down to earth. It was our landlord, who had come to inform us about a new addition to our household.

'She's a nurse, Martin. That should cheer you up! She's due back from a holiday in three weeks' time, so make her feel at home and keep the place tidy!'

I took to the idea straight away, although Emily seemed to be a little less enthusiastic. According to Emily, two women sharing the same house with one man would only lead to conflicts. I brushed Emily's concerns to one side, determined to make our new guest as welcome as possible.

Three weeks later, on a Saturday afternoon, she arrived, her family noisily helping her to move into the bedroom next door, much to my annoyance, after working a night shift. After the noise had subsided. I quickly showered and dressed, ready to go to the local shops to buy food for my tea. I knocked on my new neighbour's bedroom door. 'Come in.' I walked in and couldn't believe my eyes, as I made my nervous introduction.

'Pleased to meet you. My name is Jen,' she replied.

I hurried out of the room, after promising to show her the local sights on a future occasion. My heart pounded wildly, as I made my way towards the shops. I'd heard about love at first sight, but this was something more. I knew that I'd met this girl before, the overpowering feeling of *déjà vu* confirming this.

The feeling of attraction appeared to be mutual, as Jennifer agreed to accompany me on a night out, the following Saturday.

I spent the rest of the week, nervously anticipating our first evening together, wondering how she would react to my life-style and interests, especially the spiritual aspects, although my intuition would, I felt, intervene and come to my rescue, should the need arise.

'Have a nice evening!' shouted Emily from the kitchen, as Jen and I set off to catch the bus into town. After a brief tour of the noisy pubs and clubs, we decided to visit one of the many wine bars located in the town centre. The atmosphere was perfect, I decided, as the waiter comically danced his way through the maze of candle-lit tables, in time to the romantic music.

'Your turn now,' prompted Jen, after briefly describing her life as a nurse, full of adventures, parties and sexual escapades. Well, it's now or never, I thought to myself. Jennifer sat in silence, as I relayed my carefully rehearsed life history.

'Well, that's about it so far,' I muttered, trying to sound as confident as possible.

'That's very interesting,' began Jennifer. 'I've always tried to keep an open mind about spirituality, although some of the more bizarre aspects belong to the realms of fantasy.'

'What do you mean?' I asked, rather naïvely.

'Well, I'm not saying that I disbelieve your story, but I've never had any proof of mind over matter, or life after death.'

'Just a minute,' I interrupted, sensing the perfect opportunity for a small demonstration that would, hopefully, prove that my story contained more than a nugget of truth, and was not in any way exaggerated by the evening's alcohol consumption.

'Would you mind if I gave you a small demonstration of mind over matter?'

'Not at all. What have you got in mind?'

'Well, I've read in one of my books that Tibetan monks are able to control their heart rate, using mind over matter. You are medically trained. Is such a feat possible?'

'I wouldn't think so, for one moment,' said Jennifer.

'OK, could you take my pulse rate, if you wouldn't mind?'

'Eighty beats per minute, nothing unusual there.'

'Just one moment,' I said softly, closing my eyes and going instantly into a very deep meditation, taught to me by the earth group.

'OK, take it now.'

After 30 seconds, Jennifer's face began to pale.

'What's the matter?'

'That's impossible, your heart rate has more than doubled!'

'No, Jennifer, you're missing the point. A lot of people regard many things in life as impossible; it therefore becomes a self-fulfilling prophecy. If people would only for one moment in their life remain open to the powerful potential of the human mind and spirit, the world would definitely be a better place to live in.'

After 20 minutes spent philosophizing about the human race and the world's eventual destiny, we decided to walk home. I lay on my bed staring at the ceiling, not quite being able to believe my luck. Not only had Jennifer enjoyed our evening together, she had actually asked if we could repeat the exercise once again, in the near future.

One thing led to another and within a relatively short space of time we became lovers, spending as much time as possible in each other's company; so much time in fact, that I had begun to neglect my meditational exercises which, by this time, had become a daily routine. The fact that Jennifer and I both worked night shifts during the week didn't seem to help, until one December day in 1988 I received a letter from my solicitor, informing me that my wife had sold our property, which meant that I would receive half of the proceeds.

It couldn't have come at a better time I thought, deciding immediately to leave my job at the bakery and take time out. After all, I reasoned, I have worked quite hard up to now, without much of a break. Besides, I could kill two birds with one stone – more time for Jennifer and more time to begin in earnest with my studies, without having to worry about the financial situation.

For the first time in my life I could really taste and feel my freedom, the sort of freedom which meant going on shopping trips and actually being able to afford nice clothing, nights out and a host of other wonderful goodies including, of course, books of a spiritual nature, which seemed to be slowly but surely increasing in numbers, which indicated to me, the growing interest in matters of a spiritual nature.

The atmosphere in our household seemed to be excellent, and the addition of two newcomers didn't make any difference. Everyone seemed to share the responsibility and to respect one another, helped by the differing working hours. However, it was during one of the rare evenings when everybody was at home watching television that I made one of the biggest mistakes of my life. The programme was about dreams and premonitions and seemed to be handled from a neutral viewpoint, which surprised me greatly, as such programmes were usually treated quite frivolously by the invited scientific expert. Throughout the programme, a few examples of premonitions were thoroughly investigated and dissected by the experts but, try as they could, the scientists failed at every attempt to give a logical explanation for the sequence of events. Viewers were left to make their own minds up and my fellow housemates were soon engaged in a heated discussion about the merits of the programme. I remained in complete silence, like an observer from within, interested to know how the average person would react to such claims. Jennifer attempted to give her own meaning, and was immediately laughed at by the others. I couldn't believe that people could be so cruel and naïve and, remembering the vivid dream I'd had the night before, I interrupted the rapidly deteriorating conversation.

'Listen!' I barked out, with as much authority as I could muster. 'I will end this argument once and for all. Within a day or two, there will be a mid-air collision between two RAF jets. One pilot will be killed, the other will eject and receive minor back injuries!'

I left the room in total silence and made my way upstairs to the safety of my bedroom, closely followed by Jennifer.

'What was all that about, Martin?'

'It was just a moment of madness. I know I shouldn't have said anything, but they were laughing at you.'

'Is it really going to happen?'

'Yes, I'm almost one hundred per cent sure that it is. The dream was exactly the same as the last one, including the news report.'

'I hope so, for your sake,' said Jennifer.

I woke up the following morning, showered and dressed quickly, determined to catch the next train to Yorkshire, to visit a New Age shop which housed, according to the brochure, the largest collection of New Age books and artefacts in England. I caught the train with two minutes to spare and, following instructions, caught the appropriate bus. I couldn't believe my eyes – the shop more than lived up to my expectations, crammed from top to bottom with goodies. Tibetan singing bowls, incense, books, cassettes, various potions and meditational aids, you name it, they had it! Two hours later I left the shop, having spent much more money than I had intended, and made my way back towards the town centre. I had just missed the train and felt hungry, so ate a rather greasy-looking meal of fish and chips at the railway station restaurant. On the way home I bumped into Emily, who was on her way home from work.

'Martin, have you seen the news today?'

'No, what's the matter?' I replied, having already forgotten the events from the night before.

'What you said, last night, it's happened today!'

I was momentarily stunned and speechless, a cold sweat broke out on my forehead. I just couldn't come to terms with this news and for a moment or two, refused to believe Emily's story. As we neared home, I heard Jen's distinctive voice from behind, calling my name. I stopped to allow her to catch up and asked her if she'd seen the news today.

'Yes, Martin, it's true; it happened exactly as you described it.'

I was in a state of complete shock and couldn't believe how calmly Jennifer and Emily had reacted. I ran up the stairs, dumped my three bags on the bed, and made it downstairs just in time for the evening news and there it was, reported exactly word for word, as I had seen and heard in my 'dream'. From that moment on, the atmosphere in our previously harmonious household began to deteriorate rapidly until, after a few months, with the exception of Jennifer, I began to feel totally isolated, the others seeming to be going out of their way to avoid me.

My prophetic dreams continued unabated, occurring on average perhaps once or twice every month. The subject matter always involved air crashes, in one way or another. Luckily enough I could always confide in Jennifer and during one of our many discussions about my dreams, Jennifer asked why they always involved aircraft. I hadn't given it a thought. I'd just accepted the dreams as an integral part of my spiritual awakening, without even thinking about an explanation until one evening I decided to meditate on the problem, to see if my intuition would provide me with a satisfactory explanation.

I locked my bedroom door and carefully chose a meditational cassette which, according to the instructions, would provide the user with unlimited amounts of inspiration, and which not only strengthened your intuition, but helped in making the right decisions in difficult circumstances. Halfway through the 30 minutes meditation, as I peered through the misty haze of altered consciousness, I saw a clear picture of a telephone directory, my intuitive voice announcing, 'Here, you will find the answer you are looking for'.

After the tape had ended I lay on my bed feeling more than a little frustrated. I had actually believed the words printed on the inside cover of this cassette. I'd been well and truly taken in, I thought to myself, drifting off into unconsciousness.

The following morning I decided, against all logic, to look in the telephone directory. After all I didn't have anything to lose, apart from the knowledge that I'd been conned by the makers of the cassette. I began to thumb through the index, until I reached the letter 'C' for Clairvoyants. That's strange I thought, I can't ever remember seeing Clairvoyants advertised in a telephone directory before. After reading the advertisement, curiosity got the better of me and I telephoned the clairvoyant and made an appointment for the same afternoon.

Not wishing to be late for my appointment, I'd arranged for a taxi to pick me up 30 minutes before I was due, especially as the area was unfamiliar territory for me. The taxi arrived on time, the driver impatiently sounding his horn outside.

'What a coincidence, I can't believe it, fancy you being a taxi driver!' I blurted out to one of my former colleagues. Following ten minutes of intense discussion we had arrived at the clairvoyant's address. I said goodbye and promised to keep in touch with him, although my thoughts were firmly fixed on my first-ever meeting with a clairvoyant, wondering what on earth to expect, images of prophets of doom, dressed in black, flitting across my mind's eye. There it was, house number six. It seemed normal enough I thought, reaching up to ring the doorbell. No answer, I wonder if he's forgotten I thought, ready to turn around and leave. The door burst open.

'Hello Martin,' said the stockily built normal-looking man. 'Come in, make yourself at home, cup of tea?' By this time the stranger had introduced himself as Eric.

'Yes please,' I answered, feeling immediately at ease.

The room was full of pictures and paintings of various people, surrounded by the most beautiful colours I had ever seen.

'I'm an artist by trade,' began Eric, coming back into the room carrying two cups of tea. 'The people in the paintings are all former clients. After each session, I always find it relaxing to paint their auras. That is where I gain the clairvoyant information from.'

I sat there in silence, admiring the various paintings, while drinking my cup of tea.

'Shall we begin?' said Eric.

'Ready when you are.'

Eric closed his eyes and began to breathe rapidly in and out for a few moments, until finally coming to rest.

'What are you doing here?' Eric suddenly asked me, in a deep guttural voice.

'What do you mean?' I asked, beginning to wonder if I'd made the right decision after all.

'You don't need any advice from me – you could swap places with me right now and do a far better job, don't you realize it? I've never seen or felt an aura as great and powerful as yours. You should make use of it.'

I was completely taken aback, momentarily lost for words.

'I presume you have some questions,' prompted the figure in front of me.

Following a rapid exchange of questions and answers the session was over. Had I really been there for an hour? I thought, making myself a cup of tea at home, trying to recall everything Eric had told me.

The evidence of Eric's strange abilities was overwhelming. How on earth could a complete stranger reveal such detailed facts about my father's tragic death, my marriage and subsequent divorce, plus a host of personal details, known only to me, or so I had thought! My first doubts arose as Eric spoke about my future. According to him I would be working with cars. The only knowledge I had about cars could possibly have been written on the back of a postage stamp. The most remarkable prediction of the session came at the end.

'In answer to your questions about spirituality: it is an integral part of your destiny and you cannot avoid or escape this fact. You have probably already noticed this learning cycle, or karma as it's sometimes called. It usually takes the form of a coincidence, which eventually leads you to a person or situation, that will further your knowledge in this area. The reasons for your dreams about air crashes will be revealed to you in the not-too-distant future, when you will be more spiritually aware and able to accept the revelations. Bearing this in mind, however unlikely it may seem now, you will be emigrating to another country not too far from England, where your spiritual education will continue on a much higher level.'

I decided in the end, and after much thought, to put my visit to the clairvoyant down to experience. After all I was quite happy in England and the thought of emigrating hadn't even crossed my mind. Besides I was hopeless at languages, as my school report would testify.

The money I had gained through the sale of my house began to diminish, forcing me, much against my will, to start looking for another job. It shouldn't be too difficult, I thought to myself rather naïvely. After all I'm dependable, reliable, punctual and presentable and, what's more, I've even served with Her Majesty's Forces. What more could a future employer ask for?

Two and a half months later I received the chance I had been praying for. Out of sheer desperation I'd decided to register with a local temping agency, not for one moment expecting to hear anything more from the agency. I made my way home, worried and depressed about the situation I had got myself into. I had just put the key in the front door when the telephone began to ring. I couldn't believe it – the agency had organized an interview with a local telecommunications company that very same afternoon. I was told that if the interview was successful the company would like me to start immediately. Apparently they were impressed with my experience in the RAF.

The interview couldn't have gone better, I thought, as I sat in the company's plush waiting room, awaiting the manager's decision, sweating profusely, realizing that my whole life depended on another human being's decision.

'Congratulations and welcome aboard, Martin. Could you possibly start tomorrow?' asked the smiling manager, while shaking my hand vigorously.

'I can start now if you want!' I replied, enthusiastically, filled with emotion.

'No, tomorrow at nine will be fine.'

I rushed home full of excitement, to tell Jennifer the good news. She seemed to understand and share my enthusiasm and agreed to a celebratory drink or two, at one of the local bars. During the evening, the discussion about our possible future together soon came under the spotlight. After careful thought about the pros and cons of the idea, a joint decision was made to leave our present abode and move into our own house, a decision made simpler by the fact that I would once again have the financial security associated with my new career.

Following a somewhat nervous start in my new career as a help desk coordinator, I soon began to feel at home in this new nine to five office environment and became an integral part of the close-knit team.

All this while, Jennifer had been busy searching the advertisement columns in the local newspapers, trying to locate a suitable house to rent. We had already visited and turned down three of the houses, either because of the extortionately high rent that was being asked, or because of the general state of the house itself. We were beginning to wonder if we'd ever find the house of our dreams when, during one particularly busy day at work, Jennifer telephoned me and asked if I could finish work an hour earlier, as she'd booked an appointment to view what she described as 'the perfect house'. I arranged with the manager to make up for the lost time by working overtime.

'Good luck,' he said, as the lift doors started to close.

We arrived ten minutes early for the appointment, just in time to see the landlord's car disappearing into the driveway.

'Jennifer and Martin, isn't it. Pleased to meet you both,' said the landlord, shaking our hands in turn. 'Well, here're the keys to the place. Take your time, have a good look around. I will be back in twenty minutes.'

What a trusting man, I thought to myself opening the door. Jennifer and I didn't say a word – we didn't have to – the house was absolutely immaculate from top to bottom. Antique furniture, new carpets, fitted kitchen, bathroom with shower, beautifully kept garden, large bedroom, plus a washing machine in the cellar. It's tailor-made for us, Jennifer and I agreed excitedly, although the rent did seem to be a little on the steep side.

Two weeks later, with the help of my brother, we'd moved into our new dream home. The shortage of money didn't seem to pose too many problems at first – after all, here we were, living in our own home, both working in reasonably good jobs with our whole future ahead of us. We didn't realize then that things were about to change, and not for the better.

Unknown to us, our neighbours for those first twelve months in our new house had moved, to be replaced by the loudest and most unsociable people I have ever had the misfortune to meet. Frequent arguments would swiftly be followed by the sound of smashing plates and sometimes furniture. The situation was further exacerbated by the fact that my promised promotion at work had been turned down, due to financial constraints. I felt cheated, knowing full well that the company had made huge profits at the end of their previous financial year, and that plans were already being made for a further expansion.

Of course my work began to suffer, due to a general lack of sleep combined with the feelings of betrayal I felt towards both the company and my manager, who must have been partly responsible for my lack of promotion. My relationship with Jennifer took a turn for the worse and, after a heart-to-heart discussion, it was decided that I should leave my present job and concentrate on finding another more suitable position.

The company accepted my resignation and I began immediately to search for a new job. Because of newly introduced social security regulations, I was ineligible to claim any unemployment benefit, which meant living on one wage. I felt as though I'd fallen into a deep and never-ending dark abyss, until, after seven weeks of desperation, I remembered a book about meditation I'd received for my twenty-eighth birthday, and disregarded at the time.

Jennifer was working late into the evening, so I decided to try one of the meditational exercises, in the knowledge that I wouldn't be disturbed. According to the author, the knowledge contained within the book had been communicated to a highly spiritually developed Tibetan monk, a few centuries earlier. The exercises were to be followed to the letter, especially the breathing aspects. Failure to adhere to the instructions could lead to physical, mental or spiritual problems. Well, what have I got to lose? I thought to myself, preparing the incense ready for my meditation.

After five minutes forced and rapid breathing, I began to feel a little light-headed and, following the instructions, started to breathe normally. By this time, all body sensation had disappeared, followed swiftly by a faint but distinct buzzing noise. A feeling of light panic came over me, as I heard what could only be described as low chanting voices. I was just about to open my eyes when I was struck by a blinding flash of light; the next moment, I found myself sitting in what seemed to be a cave. Eleven or twelve monks were arranged in a circle, dressed in orange robes, chanting in an unrecognizable language. None of the chanting monks seemed to be bothered by or even aware of my presence. A tremendous feeling of peace and tranquillity engulfed my very soul. I must be dead, I thought to myself, wondering how Jennifer would react to my lifeless body in the living room.

'Hello Martin, at last we meet again,' said a male voice from behind me. I turned around to be confronted by a tall balding monk, dressed in the same strange garments as the others.

'Where am I, what's happened to me, am I dead?' I blurted out. The stranger began to smile.

'No, Martin, you're not dead. In fact you are more alive than you thought you were. My name is John; don't you remember me?'

'I've never seen you before in my life; please just tell me what's going on.'

'From this moment onwards I am your spiritual guide. If you have any questions or problems, whatever their nature, you may, by way of the same meditation, return and consult me. You are about to undergo great changes in your life, so please remember, you must remain spiritually open and aware at all times. No matter how impossible a situation or an event may seem, help is always at hand. You will soon be in a state to perform what most people would regard as miracles, and you must be prepared to accept the scepticism and criticism that follows. I know that you will probably feel burdened with the responsibility that accompanies these extra gifts, but it is an unavoidable part of your education. Yes, you will probably make some mistakes, but don't forget it is only from our mistakes that we can truly learn and fully understand. This new ability will enable you to reach people previously ignorant of such universal and spiritual laws, creating a domino effect which will eventually encompass the whole world.'

The strange monk's last few words began to fade, his well-chosen words seeming to add an even greater burden of responsibility on my already troubled shoulders, until I found myself back in the living room, still in the same position. A quick glance at the clock showed that the whole experience had lasted around six minutes. That just wasn't logically possible, I thought to myself – it felt like hours since I'd begun my meditation. I quickly flipped through the rest of the book, trying to find any examples of the situation I had found myself in, but to no avail. I must have been fantasizing or dreaming, I tried to convince myself, suddenly seeing the reality of my situation. I decided not to mention the episode to Jennifer, at least until I'd managed to find a job!

Three weeks later, following tests and an interview, I started a new job as a telephone operator, logging emergency breakdown calls for one of the large vehicle breakdown organizations. It was part time to begin with but, depending upon staff rearrangements, there was the chance of a full-time position in the future.

The relief and joy I'd felt at being given a chance to resume my working career soon began to evaporate, especially when I realized that no matter how hard I worked the chances of a full-time position, let alone promotion, were as remote as they had ever been. A feeling of impotence and frustration began to take over my life, forcing me once again, to review my life and the lessons I had learnt so far.

Here I was, 29 years of age, and what had I achieved? According to the television reports which showed successful young executives, earning very high salaries in their early twenties, absolutely nothing. Yes, I had a fantastic loving relationship with my partner, a roof over my head, we were both lucky enough to be working, but what did all this add up to? A continual and seemingly never-ending struggle, just to make ends meet at the end of every month.

This country owes me more, I thought to myself. After all, I'd been willing to lay down my life, by serving in the RAF, and for what? To be thrown on the scrap heap at the age of 29!

Christmas 1991 seemed to pass me by as a complete non-event, compared to happy childhood memories. I was still enjoying my work with the motoring organization, despite the circumstances, and soon became an accepted and (I hope) popular member of the team. The atmosphere in this tight-knit community was always friendly, and during the quieter evening shifts a discussion would soon develop, covering a wide variety of topics. During one particularly boring shift, the topic of discussion began to take on a spiritual dimension, as one of my female colleagues began to describe her near-death experience shortly after giving birth, due to a severe haemorrhage. I was fascinated as she described the feelings and events that followed. The feeling of tranquillity and peace, the warmth, followed inevitably by the journey down the tunnel, ending with the blinding white light.

I couldn't believe it – here was a relatively quiet and intelligent woman describing, almost word for word, the same experience I'd undergone, years earlier as a three-year-old toddler. The group's reactions to her experience ranged from incredulity to disbelief. One particular male colleague vehemently refused to consider that such an event could belong to the spheres of reality and began vocally to abuse and mock at the woman. This particularly disconcerting scene continued unabated for fully ten minutes, finally coming to an abrupt end with an unexpected flood of breakdown calls, leaving the aggressor and myself alone in the rest room.

'What do you think, Martin?' asked my red-faced, visibly agitated colleague.

'Well, I always like to keep an open mind on that subject,' I replied, as matter of factly as I could,

'Well, nothing like that has ever happened to me, no spiritual experiences or ghostly appearances. As far as I'm concerned, all that mumbo jumbo belongs to the realms of fantasy and science fiction.'

I felt so frustrated and angry whilst listening to the bigoted and, in my eyes, naïve reply from my colleague, that I'd already decided to challenge his negative stance towards the spiritual aspects of life.

'Listen, if I could prove to you the existence of telepathy would you, in return, promise to keep an open mind in future?'

'Yes, of course I would, but how on earth do you intend to do that?'

'Listen very carefully,' I replied, sounding more important than I'd intended. 'When we retake our positions in the operations room, I want you to select one of our colleagues – it doesn't matter which one. When you have finally made your choice, contact me on the intercom system and tell me who you have chosen.'

'Yes, but what's the point?'

'The point is, by using telepathy I will compel that person to turn around and look at me. Would you have more faith then?'

'Yes, of course I would, but that's impossible,' he replied sceptically.

Five minutes later the experiment could begin. He had already selected his subject, who sat on the other side of the office to me, busily chatting away to her friend opposite. I began to visualize the face of the woman, carefully making sure not to look in her direction, my eyes fixed firmly towards my sceptical colleague. Thirty seconds later it happened. The woman, still deep in conversation, suddenly stopped, she turned around to face me and called across the room, 'Hello Martin,' swiftly turning back to continue her interrupted conversation. I was very pleased, especially after seeing the pale ashen face of my previously sceptical work mate. He contacted me immediately, using the intercom system, barraging me with questions.

'How did you do that. This is unbelievable, please would you teach me how to do that.'

At the end of the shift, he approached me once again, asking for advice and, following a few words of warning about the subject, I reluctantly gave him the titles of several books which might be of interest to him, realizing that the final responsibility must lie with him.

Our financial situation didn't seem to be improving. In fact it seemed to worsen month by month, resulting in endless discussions and arguments between Jennifer and me. One day, completely out of the blue, she brought up the subject of emigration. What have we got to lose? I thought to myself, wondering if Jennifer was as serious about emigrating as she had sounded. Following a particularly intense conversation, we made up our minds. The next day, Jennifer bought a book crammed full of useful information about emigration within Europe. After careful consideration, we decided that Belgium presented the most opportunities for us.

A number of vitally important decisions would have to be made, including the task of actually finding work, which was made more difficult by the fact that neither Jennifer nor I could speak any other languages.

A few weeks had passed since our momentous life-changing

decision and still we were struggling to come up with a solution to the problem of finding work. One day, however, Jennifer came up with the idea of trying to gain a position as a nanny; after all, as she pointed out excitedly, 'I am a trained nurse!'

Following an intensive period of letter writing and telephone contacts with various families in Belgium, Jennifer was finally offered a position as nanny in a small country village, about twelve kilometres from Ghent. Our initial excitement and relief soon turned to disappointment, as Jennifer and I realized that the chances of me finding a job in a Belgian village were virtually non-existent.

So Jennifer telephoned the family to thank them for their interest and, with a heavy heart, declined their kind offer.

'Where does this leave us now?' I asked her, feeling a bout of depression coming on.

'Holland,' said Jennifer, staring blankly into space.

'What do you mean, "Holland"?'

'Well, a couple of years ago I visited friends in Groningen who were working and living there.'

She continued her trip down memory lane, painting an imaginary but perfect picture, of a land that seemed to be full of the freedom and opportunity we were looking for.

Three weeks later, Jennifer had been interviewed by a family from Holland, who were, coincidentally, visiting friends in England at the time. At the end of the interview, the family had promised to let Jennifer know their decision as soon as possible.

'Yes!' she exclaimed, after receiving the fantastic news. She'd been offered the position as live-in nanny for the family, starting in mid-April.

After the euphoria had subsided, it was time to begin packing in preparation for our new adventure. In order to save as much money as possible Jennifer had arranged to stay with her parents, while I'd already accepted a kind offer to stay with friends until Jennifer had settled down in her new job in Holland.

The first few weeks spent apart actually brought home to me how much I loved Jennifer. I missed her terribly, although this temporary bout of separation did give me the opportunity to review my life so far. Following days and nights of lonely contemplation, I'd decided to end my romance with the spiritual side of life. After all, what had it brought me? Nothing but false expectations and unfulfilled dreams and promises. I'd been kidding myself, I thought. All my experiences, premonitions and coincidences were just that, a collection of bizarre coincidences, nothing more.

Having convinced at least myself, I'd already sold or given away most of my paraphernalia and books on the subject. After all, I wanted to travel as light as possible, as I'd be travelling to Holland on the ferry.

Jennifer reacted with surprise to my decision to give up my spiritual education, asking me if I'd done the right thing.

'I'm certain I have. After all, it's a new start, a new beginning for us both in Holland, I'd like to wipe the slate clean and start again.'

A few weeks later following a tearful farewell hug, I received my first telephone call from Jennifer, describing the house she was living in, her work, the weather and, best of all, that she was missing me.

'You can join me whenever you're ready,' she told me. 'The family have offered to let you stay here with me, until you manage to find your own accommodation.'

I immediately handed in my resignation at work, which gave me four weeks to prepare myself, both physically and mentally, for the journey to a new land, a new life and, hopefully, a bright future.

SIX

The next four weeks dragged by, until at last the morning for departure arrived. I sat downstairs in my friends' house, suitcases packed, staring at the clock on the mantelpiece. A quarter to two in the morning. I must be mad, I thought, listening intently to the traffic outside, trying to anticipate the doorbell being rung by a colleague from work who had, with great kindness, offered to drive me to Harwich for the early morning ferry. I missed the bell of course, although it didn't seem to disturb those sleeping upstairs. I loaded my belongings into the boot of the car and shut the door of the house behind me. The journey could begin . . .

After we'd driven about 90 miles I began to feel very drowsy. Indeed, I must have fallen asleep, to be woken only five minutes later. I couldn't believe it – we had arrived in Harwich. My colleague finally dropped me off at the embarkation point for the ferry to Holland. I was really grateful for his kindness and insisted that he accepted money for his petrol costs. What a journey, I thought, as I watched his car drive away.

I boarded the ferry with time to spare, beginning to feel apprehensive as I remembered a dreadful six-hour fishing trip. What a time to be reminded of my sea sickness!

After a hastily eaten sandwich and a cup of tea, I made myself as comfortable as possible for the crossing and, after carefully reading Jennifer's instructions about the trains and connections in Holland, I drifted off into a deep and dreamless sleep.

Several blasts of the ferry's hooter brought me back to reality. I made my way to the upper decks, just as a signpost came into view, proclaiming, 'Hoek van Holland'. I collected my baggage and joined an enormous queue to disembark, looking forward to my reunion with Jennifer. The train I had to catch was already waiting at the station platform. After an anxious ten minutes with passport formalities, I bought my ticket and boarded the train just as the doors closed.

At Amsterdam I had to change trains and, with 15 minutes to make my connection, I decided to telephone Jennifer to let her know what time I'd be arriving. After ten minutes I'd given up, as all the telephones in the station were for telephone-card users only. In any case, my train arrived a few minutes early, so I climbed aboard immediately, not wishing to be later than I already was. The journey didn't last long, and before I knew it we'd arrived in Alkmaar, where the connecting train to my final destination of Obdam was already waiting. Ten minutes later I'd finally arrived, at the end of an extremely tiring 21-hour journey. Jennifer was at the entrance to the small station, waiting to greet me. I had just enough energy left to give her a hug and a kiss. After a quick introduction to her employer, my suitcases were put into the car for the short drive to Jennifer's new home in a small country village, a few kilometres north of Obdam. Jennifer's employer helped me in with my luggage, then left us to catch up on lost time.

I slept like a log until 11 o'clock the following morning. Jennifer made me a cup of tea, introduced me to the family's young daughter, then took me on a guided tour of the house. After a shower and unpacking my clothes, I was ready to get dressed for a sight-seeing trip around the village.

'Don't be too disappointed – it's only a very small town,' said Jennifer, as I left the house. Ten minutes later, I returned in a state of shock. The reality of the situation had suddenly hit me after hearing the people in the village chattering away in Dutch. Of course, I couldn't understand a word of what was being said and I had an immediate though thoroughly naïve feeling of paranoia. What on earth were they talking about? Were they talking about me?

'Don't worry,' said Jennifer, trying to calm my nerves. 'We'll go for a trip in to Alkmaar tomorrow; it's quite a large city and the chances of you finding a job there should be quite good.'

Jennifer's employers returned home from work and, after a

pleasant evening meal washed down with real Dutch beer, I sorted out the documents and papers I would probably need for the following day's job-hunting in Alkmaar.

I ended up travelling to Alkmaar alone, as Jennifer had forgotten that she'd promised to take the child to the swimming baths. I spent four frustrating hours walking around the centre of Alkmaar, under the intense heat of the blazing sun, visiting almost every agency I could find. The story was almost identical in every agency, 'Yes, your certificates and working experience are excellent, but can you speak Dutch?'

Three frustrating weeks followed and I had begun to despair, realizing that the money I'd saved was running dangerously low. I had also outstayed my welcome in the family's home. Jennifer decided that I needed cheering up and, as she had the use of one of the family's cars, organized a trip to the historic city of Hoorn.

I was completely taken aback whilst walking around Hoorn. The beautiful buildings and houses exuded a charm that belonged to a century long since gone. By the time that we reached the picturesque surrounds of the harbour, which was full of a mixture of old sailing ships and modern yachts, I'd made up my mind.

'One day, Jennifer, we'll live here,' I said, my voice full of conviction.

'You've got to find a job first!' she reminded me, bringing me down to earth. However, on our way back to the car park, I had noticed two or three agencies and decided to return to Hoorn the following week, to try my luck.

Three days and one hurriedly organized interview later, I had been offered my first job, working in a factory that produced food trolleys for most of the major airlines. The only problem was that the factory was at least 40 minutes by car from Hoorn. I assured the agency staff that I would make my own travel arrangements, desperate to hold on to the straw I'd been given.

Jennifer telephoned the tourist office nearest to the factory and arranged an appointment for me the next day, as Dutch tourist offices have a list of boarding houses in their area. The staff at this tourist office were extremely helpful and soon found me temporary accommodation with a local farming family. At last, I thought to myself, a change for the better.

The Dutch people I came into contact with were very helpful

and really knew how to make a stranger feel at home. I'd been working at the factory for only a few days when I was approached by one of my new colleagues, who'd heard about my temporary living accommodation and offered to let me move in with him, at least until I'd managed to find my own house. Needless to say, I accepted his offer and was once again on the move.

Jennifer used to drive over to meet me every evening and we usually spent the evenings exploring the scenic surroundings of northern Holland, stopping every now and then to enjoy a drink or two in one of the charming villages that dotted the flat but curiously attractive landscape.

I had just started to get used to the Dutch way of life when things took a turn for the worse. After living and working with my colleague for almost two months it became obvious that we were really incompatible and the strain began to tell. Working and living together was just not possible. So Jennifer and I started to comb the local newspapers, looking for an apartment or lodgings in Hoorn, since I had been promised a daily lift to work by an American who worked at the same factory as me. After a frustrating three weeks, I finally managed to arrange a viewing of a top-floor apartment in the centre of Hoorn, less than two minutes' walk from the harbour.

We set off early for my appointment and, after parking the car, made our way towards the harbour. The address was easy to find as the landlady's instructions were correct to the last detail. I couldn't believe my eyes: there, in the middle of a row of old cheese and beer warehouses, surrounded on both sides by a picturesque canal, stood my new home.

The landlady answered the door and, taking us up to the top floor, showed me one room. She explained that if I did decide to take it, I would have to share the cooking utensils and the bathroom with two others. I couldn't have cared less how many people I would have to share with – I was completely smitten. The room itself was quite large and the view from the window was magnificent. After discussing the question of the rent with the landlady, I agreed to move in two weeks later.

The move itself went very smoothly, since my belongings just about fitted into the car, meaning one journey instead of two. By the end of the evening I was fully installed in my new home and went with Jennifer back down the three flights of winding stairs to wave her goodbye, at least until the following evening.

I ran up the three flights of stairs in record time, deciding to listen to some music and relax on my new kingsize bed. I'd just made myself a cup of tea and switched the music on, when I heard a knock on the door.

'Martin, it's only me. May I come in?'

Recognizing the landlady's voice, I immediately turned the music down, wondering if I'd had it on too loud.

'Come in,' I said, nervously ready to apologize for the music. She came into my room and sat down.

'Listen, Martin, I didn't want to say anything whilst your girlfriend was here but the first time you came here, a strange feeling came over me, and now I'm almost one hundred per cent sure.'

'What are you talking about?' I asked.

'You're paranormally gifted, aren't you?'

'What on earth do you mean?' I blurted, wondering how a complete stranger could possibly know anything about my previous background or my experiences.

'I'm sorry if I startled you, Martin, but I've developed a strong feeling for your sort of person and near you this feeling was so intense that I just couldn't ignore it.'

I was dumbfounded.

'Listen, Martin, I can see you're rather shocked at the moment, but remember, if you need somebody to talk to about anything at all, I'll be downstairs, Don't hesitate.'

I lay down on the bed, staring at the white stippled ceiling, trying to find a logical explanation for the evening's sequence of events, remembering clearly my decision to leave the spiritual and paranormal aspects of my life behind me, in England. Yes, I thought, they had been an important part of my life, but that was now history. A history that belonged to and remained in England, and no amount of coincidences could change my mind.

The hot summer weeks of 1992, coupled with my good fortune in finding the sort of accommodation I had dreamed about, reaffirmed that Jennifer and I had indeed made the right decision to leave England. Thanks to my newly found independence, Jennifer could visit me whenever she wanted and she now spent most weekends with me in Hoorn, arriving every Friday evening at seven o'clock and returning to her employers late Sunday evening. For the first time in six months we could resume our loving relationship.

My work at the factory seemed to be going along in a pleasant and relaxed fashion until the company received a sudden glut of orders, which meant that the staff had to work longer, faster and harder to keep up with the quota. During one particularly heavy and stressful week, I arrived home at my flat completely exhausted, and decided to have a shower and go to bed. I didn't even have enough energy left to make my evening meal. After hurriedly showering and drying myself, I closed the bedroom curtains, checked the alarm clock and fell on top of my welcoming bed. One more day, I thought, then Jennifer will be here for the weekend. My eyelids began to close, releasing me from my earthly responsibilities and leading me directly down the wonderful path of unconsciousness.

Ten minutes later, or so it felt, I woke up and found myself on a country road, surrounded by mountains and hills. I couldn't understand what was going on and decided that I must be dreaming although, if this was just a dream, why could I see, hear, smell and feel everything? In my confusion I decided to take a walk down the road and take stock of this strange but very real landscape. As I turned around, startled by a distant sound, I had to shield my eyes from the strong midday sun and saw, nestling between two quite imposing mountains, what appeared to be an airport control tower, flanked on both sides by a number of smaller buildings.

Then I saw a strange-shaped aircraft which, judging by its ascent, had just taken off from the airport. Oh no, not again, I thought, realizing immediately why I'd been transported to this unknown but beautiful landscape. Less than a split second later, one of the aircraft's engines emitted an unearthly roar, followed by an explosion. The aircraft seemed suspended in the air for what felt like an eternity, before finally nosediving and crashing into a mountain side. There was a sickening explosion and flames were clearly visible from my vantage point.

The shock of being a witness to such a terrifying event sent me hurtling back towards my exhausted unconscious body at breakneck speed. My body jerked back into life on the bed, my heart pounding furiously with fear, my body drenched with a cold and clammy sweat.

* * *

Following yet another stressful day's work, I finished my evening meal in record time and was listening to music when Jennifer arrived. I went into great detail about my frightening dream, describing the terrifying sequence of events and finally made a quick sketch of the strangely shaped aircraft and the surrounding scenery.

'Well,' said Jennifer, matter-of-factly. 'If it happens, it happens, there's absolutely nothing you can do to stop it, is there?'

'No, of course not, but what's the point of it all. Why do I have to be party to and witness these aviation disasters?'

Jennifer shrugged her shoulders in answer to my question, then suggested a relaxing drink in one of the local cafes.

I'd already had enough of my work at the factory and the following morning, whilst Jennifer and I were doing our week-end shopping, I decided to buy the Saturday edition of *De Telegraaf*. Most of the job advertisements in Holland appear in the weekend editions, not in the Thursday evening editions as in most English newspapers.

We arrived back at my flat laden with shopping. Jennifer disappeared into the kitchen to make us cups of tea, whilst I flopped lazily into my easy chair and began to read the paper. My command of the Dutch language had improved enough for me to understand the main gist of the stories. I nearly fell off my chair in disbelief. There it was, on page four, under the headline 'Air Crash In Macedonia'.

The two press photographs confirmed what I'd read. The first showed the aircraft that I'd seen in my 'dream'; the second photograph sent shivers of fear down my spine. It showed a distant view of the airport control tower and it seemed to have been taken from the same vantage point as mine. Jennifer couldn't believe it, especially after I'd compared my earlier sketch with the description and photographs in the newspaper.

'Well, it looks like you're stuck with it, Martin,' she said. 'Can't you ask your landlady for an explanation? After all she did say you could speak to her about anything.'

I tried in vain to put the whole situation to the back of my mind. I just didn't want to speak to anybody about the dreams, let alone my landlady.

Why, why, why? I thought to myself, after Jennifer had left. I'd made my decision to leave the paranormal behind. I didn't even meditate any more. What kind of intelligence created these situations, completely against the will of a frightened individual. Why couldn't I be left in peace, like any other normal human being?

The dreams continued unabated until one day, completely in despair, I decided against my better judgement to consult my landlady.

'Why do you think these things are happening to you, Martin?'

'I was hoping you'd have an answer,' I replied, feeling very depressed.

'You must have some idea why. Try using your intuition.'

'The only thing that comes to mind happened in England, just after the dreams had started. Jennifer had asked me exactly the same question and a voice inside my "imagination" said something about my last life.'

It hit me like a bolt of lightning. My visit to the clairvoyant and what he had said about my previous life and the fact that I would not only be working with cars, but would eventually emigrate.

'What's the matter?' asked my landlady, breaking into my moment of enlightenment.

'Nothing,' I replied, not wishing to share this precious revelation with anyone.

'Listen, take this business card with you. It's the name and address of an aura reader. She's very good and will probably be able to shed some more light on to your situation.'

I took the card, rather ungraciously, thanked my landlady for her time and disappeared up the stairs to my new sanctuary, locking the door behind me. I needed to be alone to have time to work out logically what was happening to me.

The long hot summer continued, and now it was the end of August. Jennifer and I had already enrolled in one of the language schools in Hoorn and were looking forward to the new term, which began in September.

The teaching at the college was excellent and very soon our understanding of the Dutch language had almost doubled. Everything seemed to be going according to plan until, after one particularly frustrating morning at work, I made another one of those life-changing spur-of-the-moment decisions and left my job.

The long bus journey home provided ample opportunity for

me to try and put my situation into perspective. On the one hand, I felt very relieved at not having to return to the factory; on the other hand, how was I going to pay my rent?

Jennifer arrived at my flat the same evening and was understandably angry and upset with me, especially as we had made plans to spend Christmas in England and had already paid for the flights. She agreed to support me financially, as best she could, until I had managed to find another job.

I spent the following seven weeks travelling all over Holland, in a frustrating and fruitless search for work. Jennifer had flown to England the week before me, to spend some time with her family. The rest of the Christmas period she would spend with my brother's family and me.

I boarded the aircraft at Amsterdam, full of excitement at the prospect of spending Christmas in England, until, about halfway through the flight, I had a terrible feeling that Jennifer would not be at the airport to greet me, along with my brother and his family. I dismissed the feeling, putting it down to a mixture of excitement, imagination and the effects of the turbulence which by now had begun to toss the aircraft violently, sending a wave of fear through me. However, after some ten minutes of boneshaking turbulence, the aircraft settled down and levelled out, leaving me to breathe out an audible sigh of relief.

I wasn't able to understand my reaction to the turbulence, which I could only describe as sheer panic and fear. I had, after all, flown on a number of occasions and really enjoyed the whole experience of flight. It must be due to over-excitement added to the stress of being unemployed, I thought.

Ten minutes later, we made a perfect landing at Manchester Airport. I retrieved my luggage and, following the brightly lit signs, made my way through passport control towards the lounge area, where my brother and Jen would be waiting for me the other side of the automatic sliding doors.

'Martin!' It was my brother, who had manoeuvred himself into position at the end of the arrivals gate, ready to carry my suitcases to his car. My heart dropped immediately.

'Where's Jennifer?' I asked, knowing full well that my premonition on the aircraft had come true. My brother apologized profusely and explained that there was only enough room for one person to stay in his house. Luckily enough, Jennifer could remain at her parents. Due mainly to my financial circumstances, we managed to see one another only twice during the Christmas holiday.

So it was with a mixture of relief tinged with dread that Jennifer and I finally boarded our flight back to Holland. We were finally returning to a country that I now regarded as home. I just didn't belong in England any more, that much I knew, although what sort of future was I returning to in Holland? No job, no money to pay for January's rent, thoughts of doom and disaster filled my mind during the return flight. Following a depressing discussion back at my flat, Jennifer tried to reassure me that everything would eventually turn out all right, before finally leaving to catch the bus back to her employers.

I lay down on the bed. I had never felt as depressed and guilty as I felt at that moment and, due mainly to the anger and frustration, I decided, not for the first time, to blame God.

'You've created me and put me in this almost impossible situation, so it's down to you to rescue me!' I shouted out loud, staring at the ceiling. I finally came to my senses and quickly unpacked my suitcase, sorting out the documents necessary for the following day's job search.

My small travel alarm clock began to ring, rudely signalling the end of my troubled night's sleep. Following a quick shower and a hurried breakfast, I picked up the brown envelope containing, amongst other things, my CV, and made my way towards the centre of Hoorn, deciding to visit every single job agency in spite of my previous disappointments. Following two rather negative results, I reluctantly entered the third agency.

'Oh, you're an Englishman,' said the agency representative, with a smile, after hearing my obviously heavy English accent.

'Yes, I am. Does that make any difference?' I answered, trying in vain to mask any hint of an English accent.

'Of course not. I just wondered how on earth you'd managed to learn Dutch in such a short period.'

'What do you mean exactly?'

'Well, I have an English girlfriend and she's been learning Dutch for almost two years, and she still can't speak the language!'

After an ice-breaking discussion about our various countries and cultures, the rep excused himself and quickly disappeared into one of the back offices. Five minutes later he returned, bringing with him a freshly made cup of coffee.

'I hope you don't mind, Martin, but I've just contacted one of our clients, a compact disc manufacturer, and, if you are in agreement, you can begin tomorrow on a trial period of two months.'

I could scarcely believe my ears. Ten minutes later, after shaking my saviour's hand, I was on my way home, clutching a new envelope containing the necessary details and address of my new employers, together with an introduction letter from the agency.

I was over the moon and couldn't wait to tell Jennifer the good news. The first week back in Holland and I'd managed against what seemed to me to be insurmountable odds, to get a job. Of course, Jennifer was extremely relieved and excited by my news and we spent the rest of the evening in making future plans and fantasizing in general about the next few important years.

The work itself wasn't too bad, I'd convinced myself, even if it was unskilled manual work. What more could I expect under the circumstances? There were five of us working in the warehouse, including the foreman, who wasn't afraid to get his hands dirty and often helped out during busy periods. This created a really good atmosphere and helped to promote the team spirit. After the first few weeks I became an accepted member of the team. Once the ice was broken, I felt much more at ease and able to join in the usually boisterous conversations, which seemed to be a trade mark of the coffee breaks.

During one of the quieter periods, I'd been having quite an in-depth conversation with Bart, one of my colleagues. Halfway through the conversation I received that strange feeling of familiarity that usually preceded a *déjà vu* experience. I tried to ignore the feeling, as Bart continued with his life story, ending in the frank confession that, at the age of 24, he'd never had a girlfriend.

'Don't worry,' I blurted out, to my own astonishment. 'You will meet your new girlfriend within a month; she's got blond hair and blue-grey eyes!'

Bart stopped dead in his tracks, his face turning pale.

'How do you know that?' he stammered.

'What do you mean?' I asked, wondering if I'd somehow offended him.

It appeared that Bart already had his heart set on a girl from his local village, a girl who matched my description in full, and he was just working up enough courage to write her a love letter.

'Just a lucky guess,' I told him.

We remained silent during the next coffee break, both of us wondering, I suppose, how on earth such an uncanny coincidence could occur. From that moment on I knew instinctively that our paths were meant to cross, and that this strange episode would not be the last.

The following weeks at work returned to normality after that strange occurrence. Neither Bart nor I mentioned anything about it during our conversations until, one day, mainly out of frustration I'd decided it was time to open up and confide my thoughts to Bart. He continued working in silence as I poured out my innermost secrets about my life in England, paying particular attention to detail, especially when it came to my spiritual studies and the strange coincidences that had occurred regularly during my time in England.

After a few seconds silence, Bart turned around to face me and said, 'Why are you telling this to me?'

'Listen Bart, I only ever confide in people I feel will benefit from my experiences, and you just happen to be one of those people.'

'Please continue,' said Bart who, considering what I'd just revealed to him, remained calm and composed.

'Well, you don't have to believe one iota of what I'm about to tell you but, although you've probably not realized it, you possess the same abilities and spiritual understanding as I do.

'Listen,' began Bart, realizing that it was time to finish work, 'We'll talk some more about this subject tomorrow. I may have something surprising to tell you!'

I remonstrated with him, but to no avail. It was clear that I would have to wait until tomorrow.

The next day Bart revealed his promised 'surprise'. Apparently I hadn't been the first person to inform Bart about his suppressed and so far unused abilities. He went on to describe a series of strange events and uncanny experiences that he'd always attributed to coincidence. I tried in vain to convince him that coincidences did not exist as such, and were created consciously or unconsciously, by each and every individual on Earth, as part of their learning process. Bart immediately burst into fits of laughter and walked off, to continue working. I felt let down. Here was someone I thought I could trust, who obviously, judging by his laughter, hadn't believed a word I'd said.

I suddenly remembered my experiment with the sceptical and highly critical former colleague, whilst working at the motoring organization in England, and decided what I would do.

I confronted Bart with my plan. The warehouse we were working in contained four rather large speakers, one in each of the four corners, providing ample coverage for the whole warehouse. The stereo system was tuned into one of the larger radio stations based in Hilversum, Holland's home of radio and television.

'Listen Bart, since you've been working here, can you remember if the radio station has ever gone off the air, or suffered any kind of disruption or distortion?'

'Not as far as I can recall. Why?'

'Because I'm going to demonstrate to you, once and for all, that coincidence, in the normal sense of the word, does not exist.'

'Oh yes, how are you going to do that then?' said Bart, with more than a little disbelief.

'All right, listen carefully. It is now almost 12 o'clock. Before the end of our shift the radio station will go off the air for about five minutes. Will you believe me then?'

'Yes, of course I would, but that's impossible, it just won't happen,' said Bart, grinning confidently.

Later in the afternoon I'd completely forgotten the morning's events and was busy preparing a mail order package in the post department, when the 'impossible' happened. It was almost five minutes to three when the radio station suddenly, and without warning, went off the air, plunging the warehouse into an eerie and previously unknown silence.

Bart sprinted towards the office, to check the stereo setting, thinking of course that I'd interfered with the tuning knob. After making sure that this wasn't the case, he retuned the stereo to the still silent frequency of the radio station, turned around to face me and immediately walked off to continue working, at the same time shaking his head and muttering to himself.

I couldn't resist the temptation any longer and called out, 'Hey Bart, I did say for five minutes, remember?' And at three o'clock exactly the radio station burst back into life, with the three pips which signalled the hourly news bulletin. I felt really euphoric and spent the remaining two hours working on cloud nine.

Later that same evening, I sat alone in my flat, going over the day's strange events, knowing in my mind that the uncanny coincidences which had been an integral part of my life since my childhood days were part of my life and here to stay, despite my efforts to avoid any contact or situation involving the spiritual world. Here I was, in a foreign country, once again being confronted by people and situations which would, I knew, eventually lead to that previously unquenchable thirst for knowledge. Not only that, but today I had actually discovered that the so-called 'coincidences', could, under certain circumstances, be controlled, a feat that I'd previously considered impossible.

In the days and weeks following that incident work carried on normally and nothing further was mentioned about the occurrence until, during one of our quietest periods of the day, Bart came up to me.

'Listen, Martin, I feel I owe you an apology for the way I behaved.'

'What do you mean?'

'Well, although I didn't mention anything at the time, I believed everything you'd told me about your previous experiences. The only reason I laughed at your story was fear, the fear of a confrontation with the unknown.'

'Bart, how do you think I feel when my whole life up to now has been seemingly controlled by an unbelievable series of situations and events?'

'Yes, Martin, I understand your situation, but have you ever stopped to think why all of this is happening to you?'

At this point, I suddenly remembered the business card I'd received from my landlady, and her insistence that the aura reader was genuine.

'Of course I have, Bart, but I've never been able to find a satisfactory enough explanation, although I've got a strong feeling that I will soon have the answer.' Then I told Bart about the so-called aura reader and promised to tell him what happened.

I telephoned the aura reader in the evening, only to discover that she was fully booked for the next three weeks. I finally organized an appointment for the following month. I was slightly disappointed at having to wait for my appointment, although this point alone signified to me that the aura reader was, if not genuine, then extremely popular.

SEVEN

The next three weeks passed painfully slowly, but at last the day of the appointment arrived. After an uneventful day at work I cycled home in record time, quickly showered, changed and lay on the bed trying to relax. A last check of the map showed the quickest route and I was ready. I'd just locked my bedroom door, when I remembered the blank cassette I'd bought a few days earlier, especially for this occasion. After a panic-stricken search, I found it.

In my excitement I took at least ten minutes off what I'd calculated to be a 30-minute cycle ride and so arrived outside the aura reader's house at least 15 minutes too early. Better to arrive earlier than later, I thought to myself, plucking up enough courage to reach up and press the doorbell.

'Hello, come in!' chirped the attractive blonde woman, who, after opening the door, disappeared up a flight of stairs.

'Sit down, make yourself at home. I'll be with you in a moment,' she called from upstairs.

The strong sweet smell of burning incense relaxed my jangling nerves, as I sat down on a very comfortable settee, trying to absorb the atmosphere. She must be a very trusting person, I thought, to invite a complete stranger into her home and then to disappear upstairs, for whatever reason.

'Sorry about that Martin,' said the aura reader, as she reappeared to shake my hand and introduce herself as Caroline. 'Would you like tea or coffee?' she asked.

'Coffee will do fine, thank you.'

Two minutes later she reappeared, carrying two cups of

Martin Heald in RAF uniform. 'Date of entrance, 15 April 1980.' *(Photograph from family album)*

'In accordance with Josee's instructions, there I was, actually walking towards a large and obviously aristocratic house.' The old vicarage in Swallowfield, Berkshire. (*Photograph by Jon Stone*)

'The next moment I'd been transported back in time and had ended up outside the vicarage, standing in the garden at the back.' (*Photograph by Jon Stone*)

'The pictures were real enough, I thought, describing the beautiful river that ran through the village, including a rather picturesque bridge near where Richard used to go fishing.' (*Photograph by Jon Stone*)

'... the church where Richard's father was the incumbent had a short spire. I found this rather strange, as most of the churches in England that I could remember had tall spires.' *(Photograph by Jon Stone)*

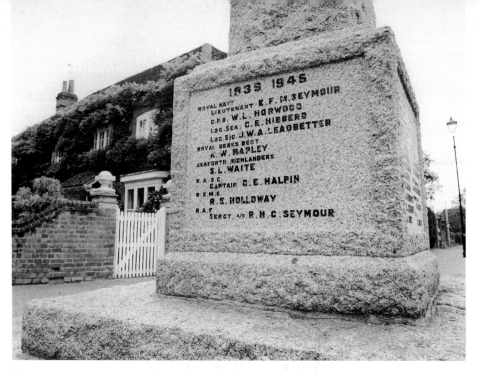

The World War II memorial in Swallowfield. RAF Sergeant Richard Seymour's name appears last on the list. *(Photograph by Jon Stone)*

'The Halifax bomber was usually manned by a crew of seven including the wireless operator who, by the use of Morse code, communicated to the home base during the long night-time raids over Germany.'
(Photograph courtesy of the Imperial War Museum)

Date of crash	:	20th July 1942
Time of crash	:	02.52
Aircraft	:	Halifax Mk II
Codes	:	W1162 NP-D
Squadron	:	158
Base	:	East Moor Yorkshire
Crashed near/in	:	North Sea 30 kms N of the island of Terschelling Netherlands
Crash due to	:	Night Fighter Oberleutnant Egmont Prinz ZUR LIPPE WEISSENFELD II./NJG2

Killed   :

Sgt Arthur Ernest WATKINS, Obs, 21, 1331702, RAF (VR)   Grave 7.C.6
Sgt Patrick Joseph DILLON, Pilot, 1378506,   RAF (VR)   Grave 7.C.11
Sgt William Henry ROGERS, Fe, 520277,   RAF   Grave 7.C.12
Sgt Herbert Edward GODFEREY, Ag (Miduppergunner), 23, 405482, RNZAF   Grave 7.E.14

Missing   :

Sgt Robert FORGIE, Ag (Reargunner), 653037,   RAF   Runnymede Panel 83
Sgt Douglas Arthur REDLER, Ab, 25, 1169796,   RAF (VR) Runnymede Panel 92
Sgt Richard Henry Creed SEYMOUR, Wop/Ag, 21, 1166511, RAF (VR)   Runnymede Panel 93

Taken Prisoner   :

Cemetery   :   Sage War Cemetery Oldenburg (Germany)

Take Off   : 23.56   Target   : Naval Yards at Vegesack.
Remarks   :
Burials were initially in the Lutheran Cemetery at Borkum.

Details collected by Mr J.G.J. de Haan, Kronenland 1432, 6605 RW WIJCHEN The Netherlands

World War II crash report '... confirmed everything I'd seen whilst under hypnosis ... in the top right-hand corner of the report was a photocopy of his epitaph which confirmed his father was a vicar.'

Martin Heald with Jennifer (left) and hypnotherapist Josee Van Asten,
pictured in England during the filming of the TV programme.
(*Photograph courtesy of* REINCARNATION INTERNATIONAL)

steaming coffee. Sitting down on an uncomfortable looking straight-backed wooden chair opposite me, she began to explain her background and how and why she'd ended up as an aura reader.

'One more thing before we begin,' she added. 'Have you got any specific questions you would like to ask?'

'Well, actually, the only reason I've come to visit you involves my last life. I don't want to go into too much detail, but I'm almost one hundred per cent sure that some thing or situation in my previous life is affecting my present circumstances.'

'All right, I shall do my best for you. Are you ready to begin?'

'Yes I'm ready. Would it be possible to record the session?'

'By all means,' said Caroline, carefully placing the cassette in an old-fashioned cassette recorder. After making sure that the cassette was indeed recording, Caroline closed her eyes and began to breathe long and deeply until, without any warning, she asked my name and date of birth. That's strange, I thought, she already knows my name and why has her voice changed? Too late now, I thought to myself, as Caroline once again repeated her question.

'Martin, Martin Heald, born 13 April 1962.'

I sat on the settee staring at Caroline, whose eyelids were flickering rapidly, and began to wonder how on earth I'd let myself be drawn into this strange situation.

'First of all,' she began, judging by the size and beautiful colours of your energy field, your life so far has consisted of a number of integrated spiritual encounters and experiences which, at first hand, seemed to be a series of completely unrelated events. I can assure you that these so-called "coincidences" were consciously orchestrated and organized, down to the minutest detail, in order to smoothe the pathway of your spiritual enlightenment in preparation for your task here on Earth. I will come back to this task later on in the session, when I will take each chakra in turn, and give you an overview of each particular colour.'

Here she paused for a few seconds, taking in deep breaths as she did so, adding. 'Any questions so far?'

'No, please continue,' I whispered humbly, after having all my previous feelings of scepticism swept away, by this total stranger's accurate description of my life so far.

'Concerning the question of your previous life, I can tell you that you are an extremely old and spiritually aware soul, with an incalculable number of incarnations behind you. Your contact with the spiritual world is deeply rooted within your soul. You must have noticed by now that you possess a number of special abilities, or gifts which, if you haven't done so already, you must be prepared to develop and make use of, in preparation for your task here on Earth. I want you to realize, without letting what I'm about to say go to your head, that you are a very special person, with an extremely important spiritual message for mankind, a message which, sometime in the not-too-distant future, will highlight a major transition in mankind's evolution upon the earth.'

The click of the cassette signalled the end of the first session. I excused myself for a moment, while Caroline turned my cassette over, ready for part two.

Caroline repeated her previous question, 'Name and date of birth?'

'Martin Heald, 13 April 1962.' The second part could begin.

'I am now receiving very clear pictures about your last life. Judging by the uniform and the surroundings, I can definitely say that it has something to do with the last World War. You are now entering what appears to be one of the old bombers and are making preparations for your mission. The next image I can see is that the aircraft you were travelling in has been shot down. There was a tremendous explosion and, although you did not experience any pain, it must have come as an unbelievable shock, to make that transition from life to death, under what I can only describe as "optimal stress conditions".'

By this time Caroline's voice was shaking with emotion and I had already decided to interrupt her moving dialogue. I realized that she'd been describing an RAF bombing mission. This sent my imagination reeling, as I hadn't told her that I'd been in the Royal Air Force during this life!

'What colour uniform was I wearing?'

'It was a sort of dark blue uniform. It must be from the Air Force, from what I could see.'

'Whereabouts were they shot down?'

'Somewhere above Holland. From what I can gather, this is one of the main reasons why you have come to live in Holland, to reclaim the energy that was left behind, after your sudden death.

'I am now being shown pictures of you as a child, in your past life. Even as a young child you'd demonstrated a number of remarkable spiritual gifts, although they seemed to remain on an unconscious level.

'Your parents were quite spiritually advanced, and were able to understand and support you with your spiritual education.'

Click! Side two of my cassette tape ended, as Caroline began to outline the fundamental colours of my energy field and their significance in relation to my spiritual advancement, adding that it would be beneficial for me to visit one of the many regression therapists based in Holland, to actually relive the experience. This should put an end to the recurring dreams about aircraft accidents.

I thanked Caroline for her advice and promised to contact her once again, should there be any future developments. I pedalled home as fast as I could in the dark, deciding to listen to the recording of the evening's events before retiring to a more than welcoming bed.

'Well?' said Bart, the following day at work.

'Well what?' I teased him.

'Come on, tell me what happened.'

I relayed the events of the previous evening and continued to prepare my first mail order package of the day, leaving Bart to mull over the consequences of my story.

'What do you think?' said Bart enquiringly.

'What do you expect me to think?' I retorted, visibly irritated, knowing full well that Bart knew what I thought. 'Try and work out the chances of a total stranger fabricating such a story that, coincidentally, involves the Royal Air Force, the Second World War and, last but not least, the "coincidence" which led to me joining the Air Force as a wireless operator, instead of my chosen trade of an electrician.'

'Yes, but what's that got to do with it?' asked Bart, rather naïvely, I thought.

'Think about it, Bart. How do you think the bomber crews used to communicate with their bases, on those distant bombing missions into Germany? Morse code, of course!'

'Yes but . . .'

'Yes but nothing,' I interrupted rudely. 'Listen, Bart, you probably won't believe what I'm about to tell you, but when I attended the Air Force recruiting office following the aptitude tests for Morse code, the officer informed me that I'd been the first person in the history of the tests to gain the full 100 per cent accuracy, and even questioned me about my knowledge of Morse code.'

It's too unbelievable for words, I thought to myself, as by now those familiar waves of *déjà vu* had returned. At that moment, I'd already made my decision. I knew in my heart of hearts that, no matter how unlikely and impossible the story sounded, there was more than a hint of truth in the aura reader's words and I would, sometime in the near future, make the effort to make an appointment with one of the regression therapists.

Jennifer and I had a number of important decisions to make, concerning the near future. Jennifer's contract as a nanny would soon be at an end. Interestingly enough, this coincided with the end of my contract for the apartment. We decided that I would begin searching for a suitable place for us both to live, enabling Jennifer to concentrate on finding herself a job.

The enormity of our tasks soon became apparent as, with June 1993 fast approaching, we found ourselves in an almost impossible situation. Jennifer would soon be unemployed. I had failed miserably to find an apartment, despite every effort.

We had all but given up hope, when one evening at the language school we were thrown a lifeline, in the shape of a friendly Russian couple who had been granted political asylum in Holland. They had been allocated a house with three bedrooms – a complete waste of space for just one couple, in their view. Jennifer and I were overwhelmed with gratitude at this hope of salvation. Following a short discussion and a visit to their large and comfortable house, we accepted their offer.

Three weeks later, with the help of Bart and his father's large van, Jennifer and I moved in with Andrei and Olga. Despite many cultural differences we soon discovered that we had much in common. Andrei and Olga were both extremely talented and artistically creative; Andrei and I even shared the same taste in music. The atmosphere in the house was fantastic, our understanding of one another bordering on a spiritual and communal level of understanding. Jennifer and I didn't want to take advantage of their seemingly boundless hospitality, however, and continued to search for an apartment of our own.

Once a week I spent an hour or so walking around the town centre of Hoorn, in the hope of finding a house or an apartment to rent. After one particularly frustrating 30 minutes I was about to call it a day and make my way towards the bus stop, when I spotted a strange-looking shop and, wondering why I'd never noticed it before, crossed the road to investigate. It turned out to be a 'New Age' shop. Why haven't I noticed this shop before? I thought, as I browsed inside. The shop was filled from top to bottom with all manner of books and artefacts, all seemingly designed with one thing in common, the quenching of my increasing voracious thirst for matters of a spiritual nature. Ten minutes and a few purchases later, I jostled my way through the crowd of late-night shoppers, just in time to catch the next bus home.

Andrei and Olga were visiting friends in Amsterdam and had arranged to stay overnight, so that Jennifer and I were alone for the first time in months. Jennifer saw me through the window of the lounge and immediately put the kettle on to make a cup of tea.

'Well, is it good or bad news?' she asked, as we sipped our hot tea.

'Both, I'm afraid. The bad news is, I couldn't find any signs of accommodation to rent; the good news is, I've managed to find a New Age shop that sells absolutely everything and anything to do with spiritual and New Age matters.'

'Yes, but how is that going to help us in our present situation?'

'Jennifer, listen. I know there's a great deal of doubt in your mind concerning my so-called spiritual abilities, but all I am asking for is a little time and patience from you and I promise that our present situation will change for the better.'

'I think there's been some kind of misunderstanding here,' began Jennifer. 'I've always believed in your abilities, right from the beginning, especially after the dreams and the coincidences which, as you've already pointed out to me, aren't coincidences, in the normal sense of the word.'

'Why on earth didn't you say that before?'

'Because I didn't want to inflate your ego; besides, I also wanted to find a job myself, on merit, without feeling that I'd somehow or other cheated another more worthy candidate, out of a job.'

'I can't believe what I'm hearing! You mean that we've been stuck in this unfortunate situation because of your pride?'

'If you want to put it like that, yes!'

'Listen carefully. My so-called abilities have nothing to do with the normal world. Thoughts and feelings such as pride and egotism form an integral part of the human psyche, but I can assure you now that they are in no way associated or connected with the spiritual side of our nature.'

'Don't make me beg,' warned Jennifer.

'What do you mean?'

'Just do whatever you have to do to get us out of this situation. I've had enough!'

'All right. Just give me 30 minutes upstairs alone. I've just bought a new meditation cassette which, according to the instruction manual, will gently guide the listener into a deeper meditational trance.'

After reading the instructions carefully, I closed the bedroom curtains, made myself as comfortable as I could on the bed and after five minutes of controlled deep breathing, switched the cassette player on.

The cassette began with the relaxing sound of crickets chirping, which then gave way to an unbelievably deep-toned vibrational buzzing sound that you would normally associate with a swarm of extremely angry bees. Within ten minutes, my body had relaxed so deeply, that any previous bodily sensations ceased to exist. I was completely overawed by this new spiritual feeling of consciousness, so much so that I could no longer hear the sound of the cassette.

I began to visualize our situation changing for the better, trying as best as I could, under the circumstances, to imagine how our new home would look. Just before the cassette ended I am certain that I could see Jennifer opening a letter and her face lighting up with joy . . .

The cassette ended abruptly, bringing me down to earth with a bump. I couldn't believe how strange I was feeling. My body seemed to have gained almost triple its previous weight.

'Well, how did it go?' Jennifer asked, trying to sound as positive as she possibly could.

'We'll just have to wait and see,' I replied, struggling to regain proper use of my faculties realizing that the cassette had indeed lived up to its claims regarding the depth of meditation.

Less than two weeks later, the impossible had happened. Jennifer had been invited to attend a first interview at a children's crèche in Amsterdam; following a second interview she was offered the position of playgroup leader which, of course, she was very glad to accept.

While she was attending the second interview I received a phone call at work from a landlord, inviting me to have a look at a wonderful two-bedroomed apartment, located in the town centre of Hoorn. I accepted his invitation, wrote down the address and arranged an appointment for the same evening. I was so excited that I'd forgotten to ask the 'landlord' how he had obtained my telephone number at work, and made a mental note to ask him later, during the appointment to view.

I arrived at the address with a few minutes to spare and was just about to ring the doorbell when a cheerful-looking man appeared on the doorstep behind me. After the usual hand-shaking introduction the landlord (for it was he) gave me a guided tour around the luxurious apartment. He told me that it would be rent free for the first two weeks, until the beginning of the next month, and that I could move in straight away if I wanted to. Of course, I accepted the landlord's offer and, just before I left, remembered to ask where he had found my telephone number.

'It's quite simple,' he said. 'My wife and I own the shop below and once in a blue moon my wife shops at the local supermarket. That's where she saw your advertisement. You're a very lucky person – that's only the second time she's visited that super-market this year.'

That's impossible, I thought, cycling the short distance home. Jennifer had placed the supermarket advertisement more than six weeks previously, and according to the supermarket rules it would have been removed after seven days, to allow everybody a chance to make use of the free advertising space.

'It's just a coincidence,' said Jennifer, but her face lit up with pure joy at the sudden but more than welcome change in our circumstances. Andrei and Olga were pleased for us, they said, although they would be sad to see us leave and asked us, more than once, if we were making the right decision.

'Listen,' said Jennifer. 'You are both more than welcome to come and visit us, anytime you want, for as long as you want.'

Once again Bart offered his services and the use of his father's van. Two days later Jennifer and I were beginning to settle into our new home, enjoying the freedom of coming and going as we pleased, combined with numerous expensive shopping trips to buy the necessities of life. We didn't even have any cutlery, let alone plates or cooking utensils. 'Those luxuries will come later,' said Jennifer. She seemed to be happier than ever before; her work at the playgroup and her new colleagues provided her with just the sort of job she'd always wanted.

So we could, at last, breathe a sigh of relief. It had taken us nearly 15 months to do it but here we were, living in our own new home, both of us in full-time employment. We could sit back and enjoy the fruits of our labours. This, combined with yet another baking hot summer, made 1993 another year to remember.

The only negative aspect seemed to be at work. The company I was working for had begun to expand, which led to an enormous increase in our small team's workload. Following repeated complaints, the management team finally relented and employed three temporary agency staff, increasing our small team to seven members. After a short working-in period, the new temporary staff were fully accepted into our close-knit community, and were even allowed to work overtime, a privilege rarely granted to agency staff within the company, because of the expense.

One particular member of the agency staff attracted my attention. Mary was only 17 and was working for the agency, in between school terms, to earn a little extra pocket money. The first time I saw her, I experienced exactly the same feelings of *déjà vu* I'd felt when I'd met Bart some ten months earlier. From that very first moment I knew that I would somehow have to steer one of our daily work chats into the spiritual domain, in an effort to gauge her reaction. Quite how I could achieve this remained a frustrating mystery, until one particularly boring day, whilst working opposite Bart, the perfect opportunity presented itself. Mary had just completed a small export order and deposited the package of CDs on Bart's table, then turned around and walked towards the office to pick up the next order slip. I made sure that Mary was still within earshot and shouted over to Bart, 'Why on earth did I choose 1962 to be born?'

Bart laughed and replied, 'You tell me!'

I grunted a half reply to Bart and shrugged my shoulders,

carefully keeping one eye on Mary who had by now picked up her new order slip and made her way towards the other end of the warehouse, without blinking an eyelid.

I felt disappointed. Either she hadn't heard my feeble attempt to attract her attention, or my intuition was, for once, completely wrong. I convinced myself that she'd probably not heard me; after all, the music had been rather loud. I decided in the end to play it by ear and should any further opportunities present themselves in the future I would try once again to make that all-important first contact.

I woke the following day, determined to forget the previous day's disappointment and complete some of the outstanding orders at work, which were already a day or two behind schedule. I buried myself in my work and had all but forgotten the incident, when Mary shyly approached me.

'Hello, Martin, I heard what you said to Bart yesterday. What exactly did you mean, about being born in 1962?'

'What are you talking about?' I replied teasingly.

After listening carefully to Mary's reply, including a startling and poignant story about her childhood, I knew that once again I'd hit the spiritual jackpot. I decided from that moment onwards to accept my feelings of intuition. How could I ever doubt its veracity? From my birth right up to the present moment I'd been shown, time after time, through a mixture of uncanny coincidences and events, a latent ability that up to now I'd chosen to ignore, despite the mounting evidence that even a sceptic would find hard to dismiss.

This meeting with Mary proved to be an important turning point in my life and shortly afterwards we became close friends, spending many hours of our free time discussing our life stories and sharing our ideas, our beliefs and encounters with the spiritual world. The main subject of our conversations always seemed to return to my encounter with the aura reader and the stunning 'coincidence', as Mary liked to describe it, of the RAF and Morse code. In the end, and following a period of goading from Mary, I promised to visit a regression therapist after Christmas. I hoped, perhaps naïvely, that she would somehow forget my promise, which had after all, been made under duress.

Jennifer and I celebrated our first Christmas in Holland together and invited numerous friends over to our house. We thoroughly

enjoyed ourselves, especially during the New Year's celebrations, when I for once let myself go, and ended up drinking
several too many, waking up the following afternoon with a
tremendous hangover. Not a very good start to the New Year, I
thought, swilling a second paracetamol down my extremely dry
throat, promising myself that I would never again repeat this
same silly mistake, whatever the occasion turned out to be.

The first few months of 1994 proved to be rather flat, certainly
compared with the exciting months of 1993, until Mary reminded
me about the promise I'd made her 'last year', as she put it, rather
unsubtly. She then proceeded to pester me for the rest of the day,
finally forcing me into submission.

I can't believe I'm doing this, I thought, as I carefully dialled
the number of the nearest regression therapist in the area, in
order to make an appointment. The therapist, who had
introduced herself as Josee, sounded cheerful enough over the
telephone and although she was fully booked for the coming
month, she agreed to fit me in during one evening in two weeks
time. I thanked her for her understanding and promised to
ring her back, should I change my mind. The chances of that
happening are very slim indeed, I thought, as a picture of Mary's
sarcastic look flitted across my mind's eye.

'Well,' said Mary, the following day at work.

'Well what?' I replied, deciding to prolong her torture a little
while longer.

After an hour of name calling and sarcastic abuse, I decided to
put an end to Mary's misery. After all, without Mary's pushing, I
don't think for one moment that I'd have plucked up the courage
to make an appointment to see the therapist.

Mary even had the audacity to arrange a lift for me, on the
pretext that, should I for any reason change my mind, I would be
forced to cancel not only my appointment, but also Bart's very
kind offer of a lift.

I had absolutely no intention of cancelling my appointment
with the regression therapist.

EIGHT

The evening of my appointment arrived and Jennifer, sensing my nervousness, wished me good luck and told me to relax and enjoy the experience.

'That's easier said than done,' I muttered, as I stood in the hallway, ready to leave. Jennifer promised to wait up until I returned and, after one last goodbye kiss, I made my way towards the arranged meeting place, where I hoped that Bart would be waiting.

'Where to?' said Bart, rather impatiently. 'I've got to attend a meeting very shortly,' he added.

I reached into my coat pocket and managed to find the therapist's address, a small fishing town about 16 kilometres from Hoorn.

'I thought this would be quite easy to find,' said Bart, as he rolled down his window to ask for directions from one of the town's inhabitants. Ten panicky minutes later, we'd arrived. I thanked Bart and promised to relay the evening's events to him at work the following day. I watched as his car disappeared into the evening mist and checked my inside coat pocket, to make sure that I hadn't forgotten to bring the blank cassette tape that I had bought specially.

'Come in, Martin,' said Josee. At first sight she appeared to be younger than I'd imagined from her telephone voice. She introduced herself and quickly took me up a long flight of stairs, into one of the bedrooms.

'It's much quieter up here, less chance of disturbance,' she smiled. 'Now, I've just made a pot of herbal tea – would you like a drink before we begin?'

'Yes, please,' I replied, surprised at the informality of the occasion, any preconceived ideas I'd had completely swept away.

Josee returned, with our cups of herbal tea, and began to explain her form of therapy. Any misconceptions I'd previously had about hypnotherapy were swept away. After I'd finished my tea, she asked me if I had any special questions about my previous life. I briefly described my meeting with the aura reader and the information that had subsequently emerged, and asked Josee if it was possible for her to pay particular attention to specific names, dates, times and places.

'I will do my best, Martin, but you must realize that it usually requires a number of sessions under hypnosis before the events of a previous life begin to emerge.

I thanked her for her advice and, after making sure that my cassette was safely recording, followed her instructions and made myself as comfortable as I could on the therapy couch, while Josee placed a blanket over me.

As I closed my eyes, I could hear her fumbling in the background and wondered what she was doing, until the relaxing music began to waft its hypnotic spell of sound around the incense-filled room.

Josee's reassuring voice was only just audible above the enchantingly beautiful music and, following her softly spoken instructions, I could feel every muscle in my body beginning to relax, until she placed her hand on my forehead. Her hand felt so warm and comforting that I felt I could stay there forever. By this time, all sensations and feelings previously associated with my body had slowly but surely melted away. All that remained was my consciousness.

This was the real me, unhindered by the almost unbearable weight of my body. I was completely free from the confines of time and space. The concept of minutes, hours and days became obsolete, as that special feeling of total and complete freedom wove an almost intoxicating spell of magic around my remaining senses.

I was so carried away exploring this new but strangely familiar world, that I'd completely forgotten where I was, until I heard Josee's faint, clear voice piercing through to the deep levels of consciousness that I'd reached.

'It is an extremely pleasant and sunny day,' she began. 'You are taking a stroll in the countryside, through a small forest, and as you make your way through the forest you can see in the distance a large house. Can you see the house?'

I couldn't believe what was happening to me. In an instant, it seemed, the darkness had been replaced by a beautifully sunny day and, in accordance with Josee's instructions, there I was, actually walking towards a large and obviously aristocratic house. Her voice interrupted my progress towards this imposing and by now brightly lit building.

'When you reach the front door, you will find that it is unlocked. I want you to go inside the house, and once inside you will notice that on both sides of the hallway there are sets of doors, stretching as far as the eye can see. When you reach this point, could you warn me.'

I felt on top of the world as I entered the house. This adventure was slowly but surely turning into an Alice in Wonderland journey, a fantasy, while at the same time it felt so real. The doors on both sides of the vast hallway seemed to go on forever, stretching out into what I imagined to be infinity.

'Now, I want you to choose the door which represents your last life on earth, open the door and enter the room.'

Following the instructions I opened one of the doors, fully expecting to see nothing on the other side. This was after all only my fantasy . . .

I couldn't believe my eyes, as I ventured further into the slowly fading evening light of a strangely familiar, large and spacious room, and began to explore and describe the environment to Josee. I started to walk around the room, trying to take everything in, while at the same time answering Josee's questions, which had begun to irritate me!

'I am now walking over a beautifully patterned carpet with different colours, mainly red and a sort of beige-cream colour. As I look out of the large windows, I can see a beautifully kept garden. There is also a large open-hearth fireplace in the room. Above the fireplace I can see a large antique mirror hanging on the wall.

'Are you a man or woman?'
'Man.'
'Are you an adult or a child?'
'Eighteen or nineteen.'
'What year is it now?'
'1938.'

Following Josee's request, I explored the rest of the house and was just about to make my way back down the stairs, when she asked, 'What is your name – your mother is calling you from downstairs – what is your name?'

I stood at the top of the stairs in tense anticipation, for what felt like hours, until I heard a familiar female voice calling out my name.

'Richard, Richard Seymour.'

'Which country do you live in?'

'England.'

'Whereabouts in England?'

'Somewhere near Oxford.'

'Are you still at school?'

'No, but I'm studying at home.'

'What does your father do?'

'He is a vicar, he works for the church.'

'Is he rich?'

'Rich enough.'

'What year are we in?'

'1938.'

'How old are you?'

'Eighteen.'

'Good, I want you to go forward in time, until something important happens.'

The next moment something very strange occurred. One minute I was standing quite happily on the stairs in the house, the next minute I'd been transported through time and space, and found myself trying on an Air Force uniform. It wasn't a particularly good fit, and the material seemed to irritate my skin.

'What's happening?' prompted Josee.

'Uniform, it's too heavy.'

'The uniform is too heavy for you?'

'Yes.'

'And then?'

'Lots of shooting, military exercises.'

'A completely different life than you were used to?'

'Yes, absolutely.'

'What happened next?'

'I was chosen.'

'What were you chosen for?'

'To learn the Morse code.'

'And then?'

'I've got to move to another camp.'

'What do you think about that?'

'Not much.'

'Good, I want you once again to go further in time, until the next important event.'

There it was again. The memories faded into an all-pervading darkness, followed almost immediately by the next set. I was beginning to wonder if I had any control at all over this strange situation.

I suddenly found myself sitting on a distinctly uncomfortable chair, in what appeared to be an aircraft hangar full of people. Everybody seemed to be joking and laughing, in between gulps of steaming hot tea. As I began to take stock of this new situation, I recognized friends and colleagues of mine, all deep in animated conversation, followed swiftly by bouts of uncontrolled laughter.

'What are you thinking about?' interrupted Josee.

'My friends, they are all laughing and joking.'

'Don't you share their happiness?'

'No, I've had a premonition about what's going to happen to us, but I can't tell the others.'

'What's going to happen?'

'Death!'

'Does this have anything to do with the War?'

'Yes.'

'How does this make you feel?'

'Very sad, seeing my friends for the last time.'

'Only you knew what was going to happen?'

'Yes, but how could I possibly tell my friends?'

'Have you lost many friends?'

'Not really close friends, more like colleagues than friends.'

'Good, I want you to go forward in time, to the next most important event or situation.'

Once again the same strange sequence of events followed, only this time I found myself under quite a different set of circumstances.

There I was, sitting on the left-hand side of an extremely loud and noisy aircraft, staring at what appeared to be an old radio set. The distinct feeling of being in flight, together with the dingy and dark surroundings, made it an eerie scene, almost surreal.

I was straining my eyes to look around, when one of my colleagues, who had been deep in conversation, began to shout out instructions to me, although the noise of the aircraft's engines drowned his message completely. I was just about to ask him to repeat his message when Josee's familiar voice broke in.

'What's happening now?'

I couldn't believe the situation, and was so confused that I didn't know who to speak to, Josee or my colleague, who at this point had begun to shout even more loudly, in order to attract my attention.

'I want you to go further on in time and describe to me what happens.'

'Lights, very bright lights.'

'And then?'

'The aircraft's being buffeted, we're being attacked!'

'And then?'

'Explosions.'

'And then?'

'Complete darkness, nothingness.'

'Has the aircraft been hit?'

'Yes, from below.'

'Are you still alive?'

'No.'

'Can you see your body anywhere?'

'No, it has been completely burnt up.'

'And you yourself?'

'Lost, confused, what happens next?'

'Are you frightened?'

'No.'

'Do you understand that you are dead?'

'Yes.'

'Good. What happened next, did anyone come to meet you?'

'No.'

'Nobody at all?'

'Yes, a light, extremely bright light.'

'Are your parents still alive?'

'Yes.'

'Will there be a lot of grieving for you?'

'Yes.'

'What was your task in this life?'

'To be prepared to make sacrifices, even my own life.'

'What is your task in this life?'

'To complete the work I'd started in my last life.'

Josee decided to end the session and in a sort of reverse order counted me slowly back into normal consciousness. She ended by telling me that I would at first find it difficult to move, and to try and wiggle my fingers and toes.

Nonsense, I thought, until I tried in vain to influence my body's movement. It took me fully ten minutes before I could actually stand upright. It was then that I realized just how deep under hypnosis I'd been.

Josee and I had a brief conversation, then she took me to the local railway station. I promised that I would contact her again, should I feel the necessity for another session. The train journey home was a complete haze and seemed to pass by in minutes, rather than the half hour that it actually lasted. My mind was elsewhere, as I once again relived those final and fatal moments of my last life.

The next few months following my regression were spent in a fruitless attempt to establish the existence of Richard Seymour. I wrote to and telephoned most of the associations concerned with information about the Second World War in all its aspects. The answer I received in most cases was we're sorry but if you could give us more detailed information, such as the squadron number or his service number, maybe we will be able to help you.

The whole episode slowly but surely became an obsession, especially as I knew that the events I'd recalled under hypnosis were real events, and not in any way based on a fantasy story.

During one of our many coffee breaks at work, the subject of music was discussed. I mentioned my liking for experimental music and this led to Marcel, one of the quietest individuals I'd ever met, offering to take me to a discotheque at the weekend, explaining that Saturday night's special theme was to be experimental music. A feeling of dread came over me, as a picture of the jam-packed discotheque flashed before my eyes. I'd still not managed to defend myself against the cooped-up emotions which usually reached fever pitch in such establishments.

'Come on, you'll enjoy it,' said Marcel, doing his best to talk me into submission. 'Well?'

'I suppose so,' I replied, deciding to face and perhaps overcome my fears.

'Enjoy yourself,' called Jennifer, as I made my way down the stairs to answer the front door to Marcel.

'I'll try,' I replied, resignedly.

'Well, where exactly is this discotheque?'

'Oh, it's just the other side of the airport,' replied Marcel. 'We'll be there in half an hour.'

As a foretaste of the evening's entertainment Marcel placed a cassette into his stereo system and proceeded to turn the volume up, rendering any further conversation impossible.

'You're quiet, what's up?' shouted Marcel, above the deafening music.

'I can't even hear myself think.'

'Sorry.' And Marcel switched the music down to a more acceptable level.

We'd just ended one of those boringly meaningless conversations concerning the weather and life in general as we were passing one of the runways at Schiphol Airport. I stared at the runway, trying to think of something meaningful to say, when a picture flashed across my mind of an aircraft just missing the motorway and crash landing in the field next to the runway. The scene I'd witnessed in that split second seemed so real that I decided to mention it to Marcel as a sort of joke.

'Hey Marcel, the runway is so close to the motorway. Imagine if a pilot mistook the lights on the road for runway lights.'

'It's never happened before.'

'Well, there's a first time for everything.' But I hoped that my 'daydream' would remain just that, a 'daydream'.

We soon arrived at our destination and, despite my initial misgivings, I did enjoy myself, until, that is, waking up the following afternoon with a king-sized hangover.

'There's been a plane crash at Schiphol,' said Jennifer, as she brought me a welcome cup of coffee.

'You are joking! Aren't you?'

'See for yourself,' she replied, quickly tapping in the appropriate teletext number.

A cold chill ran down my spine as I read the report on the

television. The number of the runway was mentioned, although I wasn't sure if it was the one next to the motorway until the following news bulletin and, sure enough, there was the wreckage, exactly as I'd seen it the previous night.

'You've had these premonitions before. Why are you worried?' asked Jennifer perceptively.

'Because I told Marcel, or rather made a joke of it.'

'Don't worry – he will probably have forgotten by tomorrow and, anyway, he is rather a sceptical type, isn't he?'

I arrived at work the next morning, having already decided not to mention anything about Saturday night, but it was too late. Marcel had already told the story to everybody in the warehouse.

'I'll pour you a coffee. You just sit down and relax,' said Bart.

'What's all this then?' I stammered, wondering what was going on.

'We've heard about Saturday.'

'What about Saturday?' I asked, trying to bluff my way out of the situation.

'I've told them about the plane crash,' said Marcel apologetically.

'Just a coincidence, that's all.'

'Come off it!' The time signal for work sounded, rescuing me from what was fast becoming a potentially sticky situation.

Within a week, my colleagues had all but forgotten my 'coincidence', except for Bart, with his constant taunts.

'Coincidence, that's a laugh,' he repeated day after day until I couldn't take it any longer.

'Look, what exactly are you trying to achieve,' I snapped.

He stared at me with a sheepish look on his face. I apologized for snapping at him and explained how I'd felt when my 'daydream' had become a nightmare of reality. 'I just don't feel like talking about it and, anyway, I couldn't even begin to explain it, so what's the point?'

'Well,' he began, 'I was only curious to know if you have these premonitions on a regular basis.'

After a brief discussion, I promised to let Bart know should I be party to another 'dream'. As fate would have it, he didn't have to wait too long!

*   *   *

We'd had a particularly hectic week at work, so hectic that I'd decided to go to bed before Jennifer. I couldn't even remember getting into bed, let alone falling into the deep sleep I suddenly found myself in, until the distinct sound of voices woke me up with a start.

Why me? I thought, staring out of the aircraft window into the darkened night sky. I was sitting on the left of the aircraft occupying a window seat and decided immediately to ask one of my fellow passengers what was going on. Several minutes later I'd given up. I couldn't move my body an inch although I could turn my head to the left and right. I'd just about resigned myself to my fate when two stewardesses walked past my row. 'Excuse me,' I shouted, but to no avail; they either hadn't heard me or couldn't see me.

I peered through the gap between the seats directly in front of me and tried to listen in on the animated conversation between a middle-aged man and what appeared to be his daughter. What language is this? I thought to myself, as the girl burst into fits of laughter. It was definitely one of the eastern European languages, maybe Hungarian.

The two stewardesses were on their way towards the front of the aircraft when disaster struck. Without warning the aircraft suddenly nosedived, sending that terrifying feeling of G force through my 'body'. I felt and saw the panic and terror on the passengers' faces as the aircraft plunged towards the ground. Luggage and people were being thrown around like rag dolls in a spindryer. Seconds before the actual crash, I was plucked from the doomed aircraft at breakneck speed and woke up sweating profusely, my heart beating at a furious pace. Feeling rather faint, I made my way down the stairs where Jennifer sat watching television.

'What's the matter?' she exclaimed.

I explained my 'dream' in detail, while Jennifer made me a cup of tea.

'Is there nobody you could warn?' she asked.

'The worst part about it is the fact that nobody would take me seriously. Anyway I didn't even understand the language never mind know the flight number!'

I told Bart about the 'dream' the very next day, and also told him that I thought the aircraft was Hungarian.

Nothing appeared to happen and so a few weeks later Bart began to tease me at work.

'What a load of rubbish. You've made it all up.'

'Listen, I'm really relieved that this "dream" hasn't come true. Try and imagine what it must feel like to be on such a flight, knowing that you have only got a few seconds to live.'

That evening I arrived home and decided to relax for ten minutes before making a start on the evening meal. I switched on the television and started to look through the day's headlines on the teletext. My heart missed a beat when I saw the headline: Russian airliner crashes in Siberia.

The accident had, in fact, happened some weeks previously, but because of the Russian reporting restrictions had only just been released to the media.

The flight recorder had been recovered and it emerged that the pilot had given control of the aircraft to his 12-year-old son while he visited the toilet. The description of the sudden nosedive fitted in perfectly with what I myself had been witness to. A cold, eerie feeling came over me as I recalled the 'dream' and tried to imagine the intense sadness and grief that the victims' families and friends must be feeling.

'What am I supposed to do?' I sobbed, looking towards the ceiling, hoping for some kind of inspiration. 'If I can't stop these events from happening, I don't want to see them any more,' I added, feeling very guilty and totally frustrated at the situation.

'It's something I've got to work out for myself,' I replied in answer to Bart's probing questions at work the following day. 'And anyway, why are you interested? You didn't believe me in the first place.'

Bart shrugged his shoulders and continued his work in silence, knowing full well that if I couldn't explain the situation then how could he?

NINE

Times and people, it seemed, were changing, especially in the world of work. Mary had been transferred to another warehouse belonging to the same company, and Bart had at last succeeded in finding himself another job, nearer to his home village. Bart and I agreed to keep in touch and arranged to have a drink, to celebrate his good news. During the evening's celebration, and probably due to the alcohol consumption, Bart told me that he and Naomi, his girlfriend, were very much in love and had actually tried to obtain one of their local council houses, to no avail. Apparently they had even attended a council housing meeting and the chances were that they would have to wait for a minimum of 12 months.

I looked across at the resigned-looking face staring back at me and suddenly remembered the uncanny episode with the radio, whilst Bart and I were working together.

'Listen, Bart, you don't have to wait for 12 months. I could help you if you wanted.'

Bart laughed. 'How on earth can you possibly help? The waiting list is at least twelve months long.'

'Well,' I said, grinning confidently. 'Remember what happened to the radio at work?'

'Yes, but surely . . .'

'But nothing! If you want me to help you, all you have to do is ask.'

'All right, I'm asking. I'd be more than grateful if you could somehow speed the whole process up a little bit.'

'Try to be a little more open and positive. You will receive news concerning your new house within a month from now.'

'We'll see,' said Bart.

Upon reaching home, I made myself a cup of coffee. I couldn't believe what I'd actually said to Bart. Yes, I thought, the strange influence I'd had on the radio had definitely happened – that was a fact – but this was a completely different kettle of fish. How on earth could 'I' possibly influence a housing committee, not to mention the 12-month waiting list. The only idea that I could come up with was a meditational visualization. I'd read somewhere that visualization could, in certain cases, speed up the process of materialization, but 12 months was surely asking too much. Maybe this time I'd bitten off more than I could chew. What the heck, I thought, surely Bart didn't take my proposal seriously. Anyway, if he does telephone me in a few weeks' time, to question me about his new house, I can always put the whole episode down to an alcohol-induced joke!

The week following Bart's celebratory evening, Jennifer was working late one evening and this gave me with the perfect opportunity to carry out my visualization for Bart.

After making sure that I wouldn't be disturbed, I lay down on the bed, and making myself as comfortable as possible I was armed with my cassette player and one deep-meditation cassette.

Thirty minutes later the tape finally ended, although the pictures of Bart and Naomi's happy faces, after receiving notification about their dream home, remained. Well, I thought to myself in consolation, I've done my best – either it happens or it doesn't.

Less than two weeks later, the miracle, as I'd begun to view the task, had already happened. Bart had received a notification letter from the local housing office and there they were, packed and ready to move into their new home. Of course, Bart was completely dumbfounded, as was Naomi, who by this time had been told about the incident with the radio.

I felt on top of the world! Not only had I performed what I myself regarded as a miracle, but at the same time I'd contributed to my friends' happiness.

*   *   *

The next three or four weeks, I wanted to spend alone, if at all possible, apart from my beloved Jennifer of course. I felt an urgent need to contemplate and try to assimilate the events of the recent few months. On more than one occasion, I know, I drove Jennifer to the edge of despair with my constant questioning about the strange sequence of events.

'It's just a one off,' she said, trying in vain to satisfy my burgeoning curiosity.

'I only wish it was,' I replied, remembering some of the other occasions when I'd somehow managed to exert a seemingly invisible and unstoppable influence on people as well as objects. As fate would have it, I didn't have to wait very long for another opportunity to test my newly discovered ability.

I had apparently offered to help Bart and Naomi paint the inside of their house. After the first morning's painting, Bart drove the three of us around to Naomi's sister's house for lunch. Following the usual introductions, the four of us sat down to a pleasant and filling meal. After we'd eaten, I decided to go and sit out in the sunshine in the back garden. Julie, Naomi's sister, came to join me and sat down on the garden stool opposite.

'Listen,' she began, a little self-consciously. 'I hope you don't think I'm being rude or a little too forward, but I've heard stories about you.'

'Oh, what sort of stories?' I replied, knowing full well what she was talking about.

'You know what I'm talking about, that "thing" about Naomi and Bart's house.'

'Yes, please do go on. You needn't feel embarrassed.'

Julie then went on to describe an accident she'd had at work almost a year previously. A heavy object had fallen down a set of stairs and landed directly on to her shoulder, leaving her in a great deal of pain. After frequent visits to hospital, it was finally decided that she should undergo surgery, to try and correct the misplaced bone in her shoulder.

'I have to take pain killers almost every day, the operation itself has already been cancelled once, due to the waiting time to see a specialist, and only last week I received a letter telling me that I would have to wait for at least another few months for the operation. Please, if there is anything you could do for me, I would be eternally grateful.'

I took one look at the tearful young woman, and without a moment's hesitation said: 'You will receive news regarding the operation within two weeks from now. Try not to worry about the waiting time, just trust my words.'

Julie hugged me and thanked me for listening, adding that she would telephone me instantly, if and when she received any news.

That evening, when I arrived home, I explained the situation to Jennifer, who began to question my judgement, especially in such emotional circumstances. However, after we had finished our evening meal, I arranged with Jennifer a period of 30 minutes when I must not be disturbed. I then performed exactly the same meditation as before, only this time incorporating the new set of circumstances.

The emotions from that meditation, coupled with the visualization of Julie entering hospital for her operation, were still quite fresh in my mind when, less than a week later, Bart telephoned me to say that Julie had received the necessary notification for her operation to proceed and would be admitted for surgery within the next few days. Excitedly, I relayed the telephone conversation to Jennifer, who sat down in stunned silence, as the realization dawned that these strange occurrences were not in any way, shape or form one-off events.

A few weeks later, after the dust had settled following Julie's operation, I began to think long and hard about the uncanny and almost unworldly events that had taken place in my life, since we had moved to Holland. I found it difficult to come to terms with what had happened; the list of 'coincidences' and discoveries read like a story line from a children's fairy tale book, especially when I recalled my firm decision to end my obsession with all things spiritual or paranormal.

The realization of my situation hit me like a ton of bricks. I had little or no control, let alone choice, in these matters. I had tried once, and failed miserably, in a vain attempt to avoid all contact with anything or anyone with a spiritual nature. The only question left in my mind was, what's next?

The year has passed so quickly, I thought, while browsing through the August edition of one of the local free papers. I flipped through the usual mix of news and advertisements until one particularly interesting looking advert caught my eye. A local spiritual development school was offering a new course in September 1994: '*Magnetiseren* – Everyone Can Learn It!'

My interest was further aroused when I began to read the syllabus placed next to it: 'Subject material will include, amongst other things, *Magnetiseren*, Auras, Telepathy and Meditational Exercises.'

This was it! I thought, exactly what I'd been waiting for! A chance to learn and to develop new abilities and, who knows, maybe even to find a few answers as to the reasons why I'd been selected, or so it seemed, to receive these so-called extra gifts.

I memorized the telephone number of the school. What have I got to lose? I thought, while dialling the school's number. Then followed a brief but interesting conversation with the teacher at the school. I gave him my name and address so he could send me the course enrolment forms.

'It sounds to me as though the course was tailor-made for you,' said Jennifer, after listening to my somewhat exaggerated description of the course work.

'Well, who knows?' I began. 'I might even be able to obtain some answers to my increasing list of questions about my own spiritual development. After all, they must know what they are talking about – they're the experts!'

Cycling towards the school for my very first evening of lessons, I thought how strange it was. I had all but forgotten the regression and the months of frustration and torment after-wards, due mainly to the remarkable chain of events that had followed. I began to wonder if there was any connection between my first hypnosis session and the sequence of situations and events that had taken place in the weeks and months that followed. No, I tried to convince myself, there couldn't possibly be a link. It's just too much of a 'coincidence'.

At last I arrived and was staring at the number board of a rather large and plush-looking farm house. I parked my bicycle outside and made my way towards the entrance. A quick glance at my watch told me that I was at least 20 minutes early.

'Hello there,' said a rather jolly-looking middle-aged man, reaching out to shake my hand. 'My name's Ian, pleased to meet you.'

I introduced myself, and was just about to sit down when the rest of the group arrived all at once. After everyone had helped themselves to coffee and taken their places, Ian introduced himself to the group as a whole and began to outline the aims of the course itself. Finally, he announced that we should each introduce ourselves to the rest of the group, explaining a little about our various backgrounds and giving the main reasons for wanting to attend this particular course.

I panicked, wondering what on earth I was going to give as my reasons for attending the course, before finally deciding that truth is always the best policy. After listening intently to the first two speakers, it was my turn. Four adrenalin-filled minutes later I'd finished my own introduction and retaken my seat, full of relief that I'd survived the ordeal.

The lesson itself passed by without further incident. At the end it turned into a general discussion about the varied and sometimes unbelievable worlds of spirituality. I had just put my coat on, ready to leave, when Ian took me to one side, away from the rest of the group.

'Listen, Martin, the school itself has booked a stall at a local spiritual exhibition this coming weekend. I think you would find the experience worthwhile. You could spend the day on our stall and even offer advice to the general public if you wanted to.'

I was flattered by Ian's generous proposal; after all, we had met for the first time only a couple of hours before. After I had gratefully accepted his offer, Ian handed me a small pamphlet with the address of the spiritual exhibition centre.

'I'll meet you outside the entrance to the building, at 11 o'clock on Saturday morning,' he said. I said my goodbyes to the remainder of the group, who were still deeply engrossed in conversation.

I couldn't believe my luck. Once again 'coincidence' had opened up a new path for me. I relayed the evening's events to Jennifer as soon as I got home. Her first reaction took me completely by surprise.

'Why on earth don't you begin for yourself?' she said seriously.

'I haven't even given it a thought,' I replied.

'Well,' she went on, 'if I possessed your talents and abilities, I'd certainly begin on my own.'

'I've still got a lot to learn and, besides, on Saturday I will have more of an opportunity to gain first-hand experience.'

'All I meant was, if you are thinking about starting for

yourself, you don't have to worry about financial matters. I will do my best to support you.'

I hugged her and thanked her for her advice, although my thoughts were already firmly fixed on Saturday's spiritual exhibition, whatever that entailed!

Saturday duly arrived. I almost collided with Ian outside the entrance to the exhibition centre. He was carrying various pieces of paraphernalia necessary for the school's stall at the exhibition. After two journeys between Ian's car and the building the stall was almost complete, when the head of the school arrived and introduced himself to me as Mark.

The day began with the ritual cup of coffee and a discussion about the day ahead. In the meantime the hall itself was filling up rather nicely. I watched intently as the growing crowd of curiosity seekers formed rather haphazard-looking queues to have their palms read, their auras drawn, the tarot cards read – you name it, they queued for it! There was a seemingly endless list of different disciplines to be consulted and many stalls, which offered, amongst other things, crystals, stones, brooches, meditational cassettes and home study courses, all with the same motto, 'Spirituality'.

The rest of the day turned out to be a bit of an anti-climax, since hardly anyone seemed to be interested in our stand. At the end of the afternoon, Tom, the third member of the school's teaching staff, came over to me and said, 'I hope you won't be offended by what I'm about to tell you, but I can't hold it back any longer.'

This sudden statement came as a bit of a surprise, as Tom had hardly spoken a word all afternoon.

'What do you mean?' I asked him.

'Well, you can stop me if I'm wrong, but I'm not usually wrong in these matters.' He then began to sketch a surprisingly accurate picture of my life history, from my childhood right up until the present moment.

'Am I right so far?' he asked.

'Yes, right down to the last detail,' I said faintly.

He continued with a description of the various spiritual guides who had accompanied me throughout my life so far. 'You do realize that you are clairvoyant, don't you?'

'I suppose so.'

'You suppose so! You must have made use of this gift on more than a few occasions. It's written all over you.' Tom then paused for breath, turned to face me and said, 'Although you probably may not be aware at this stage in your development, you have an inbuilt and totally natural gift for mediumship, plus a host of other spiritual gifts which will, when the time is ripe, reveal themselves.' He ended his startling but accurate revelations by saying that I should trust my intuition implicitly and 'coincidence' would take care of the rest!

'He's good isn't he?' prompted Ian on the way home. No doubt he realized the reason for my silence.

'Is he always right, Ian?'

'Well, put it this way. I've known Tom for nearly three years now and his statements have always been vindicated by the passage of time.'

Ian dropped me off outside my front door. I thanked him for the day's experience and said that I would see him the following Wednesday evening for our second lesson.

When I told Jennifer about Tom's revelations, she just smiled and shrugged her shoulders. Well, I thought, it's a good job that I can always rely on Jennifer to bring me down to earth; I'd have probably ended up going round the bend, if it hadn't been for her.

The next weekend, Jennifer and I had one of our usual Sunday lie-ins, until about 11 o'clock, when the sound of the telephone shattered my deep and pleasant slumber. I hurried downstairs to answer it.

'Hello there,' said a strange male voice at the other end.

The voice belonged to an acquaintance of Naomi, Bart's girlfriend. He explained that he was a spiritual meditation tutor and Naomi just happened to be one of his pupils. Naomi, it seemed, had told her tutor about my exceptional abilities.

'I've been in this line of spiritual learning for five years now, and not once have I come across anyone with your abilities,' he went on. 'Do you mind if I make an appointment to come and see you?'

'No, not at all,' I said, feeling really rather flattered that such a knowledgeable spiritual teacher wanted to make an appointment to see me! Arrangements were made for our meeting the following Tuesday evening.

*   *   *

The meeting itself was a strange affair. After we had exchanged brief histories, Willem finally confessed to having a small problem that he thought I might be able to solve.

'What is it then?' I asked, intrigued by the whole situation.

'Well, to put it in a nutshell, I've met and fallen in love with the person I consider to be my ideal partner. Unfortunately, she lives on the other side of Holland.'

'What's the problem there?'

'After a year or so of our long-distance relationship I decided to sell my house and move nearer to her, and that is where the real problem lies. My house has been on the market for quite a while now, and is still not sold. Do you think you could help me at all?'

I was completely taken aback! Here, in front of me, sat a complete stranger who was asking for my help. After regaining my composure I promised to meditate for him, and told him that he should hear the positive news he had been waiting for within a month.

Willem thanked me profusely for my time, and on the way out he insisted that I accepted some money for my efforts. I tried to refuse, but he stubbornly deposited some money in one of our savings tins, adding that he would telephone me immediately if he received any good news.

'It looks like I was right,' said Jennifer. 'You will be starting up for yourself after all!'

'Not at all,' I replied, naïvely. 'Besides, I had absolutely no choice in the matter and, anyway, surely he can't expect me to sell his house for him. I'm not an estate agent!'

Despite my initial misgivings, I carried out the meditation for Willem on the next Wednesday evening, after I'd returned home from the second lesson of the *Magnetiseren* course. The subject, of course, was 'Meditation'!

A week or so later, when I'd almost forgotten about Willem, he telephoned me to say that his house would shortly be sold. His gratitude knew no bounds. I replaced the handset, after wishing Willem good luck for the future, and immediately went upstairs to lie down.

This can't possibly be happening, I thought. Once or twice, yes, I could accept as luck or 'coincidence', but now the whole situation was getting completely out of hand. These 'miracles' were surely only reserved for highly advanced spiritual beings, not for an ordinary person such as myself . . .

The *Magnetiseren* course had so far failed to provide me with any satisfactory explanations, and I began to wonder if I had made the right choice after all. The first two lessons had degenerated into general group discussions, although the third lesson sounded promising enough. We were to be given our first 'hands on' experience of *Magnetiseren*.

After coffee had been drunk and the chatter had died down, Ian began to explain the basic techniques of diagnosis, paying particular attention to the chakras and where they could be located on the body. According to him, it was possible to feel the energy stream emanating from the chakras. He continued with a quick demonstration on one of the students, followed by a reasonably accurate outline of how the person was feeling.

Now it was our turn. The group split into five groups of two, each person taking it in turn to be *Magnetiseur* and patient. I was paired with one of the quietest women in the group and, following Ian's instructions, I closed my eyes and began to feel for the chakras.

I couldn't believe what was happening and wondered if I was in any way fantasizing. As I ran my hands over the chakras I could feel a sort of prickly electrified heat emanating from these energy centres, although nothing could have prepared me for what was about to happen.

I'd started checking the subject's energy centres from the top of her head, working my way slowly down to the bottom, and just as I had reached two of the lower chakras I received what felt like a jolt of electricity through my whole body, followed immediately by what seemed to be a violent and disturbing film, of a young child being subjected to all sorts of physical and mental abuse. The sudden shock made me open my eyes, just as Ian indicated that the roles should now be reversed.

At the end of the session, Ian asked each of us individually to describe our experiences and feelings. I couldn't bring myself to describe what I'd actually seen and felt; it would have been too embarrassing, not only for me but also for my partner who, I could see, was still quite shaken and unnerved by the whole experience.

Towards the end of our lesson, following the group

meditation, Ian asked if we would each bring a photograph of a friend or relative with us for the next lesson. This was to be on the subject of psychometry and would include a psychic reading of the person in the photograph.

'Don't forget to ask the person's permission,' warned Ian, as we made our way out into the misty October evening, most of us an experience richer!

The weekend came as a welcome relief, although the experiences of Wednesday evening were still haunting me. Jennifer and I had cooked a special English-style Sunday dinner, with roast potatoes, beef, vegetables and all the trimmings. We were just about to sit down at the table when the doorbell rang.

'Who on earth can this be?' asked Jennifer. 'I'm not expecting anybody.'

When I opened the door I was surprised to see Naomi's sister Julie, together with her mother and brother.

'What on earth is the matter?' I asked Julie, whose face was blotchy and tear-stained. I invited them inside and gave them all a drink, then returned to the dinner table. Julie explained that she'd found her cat dying outside her house with no obvious signs of a wound. They had just returned from the emergency vet, who'd said that the cat had somehow been poisoned, and the only thing he could do was administer a pain-killing drug although its chances of survival were minimal.

'What do you expect me to do?' I asked, suddenly feeling totally out of my depth in such an emotional situation.

'I know you possess paranormal abilities – you've already demonstrated them on a number of different occasions.'

'Yes, that's as maybe. But I've got absolutely no experience with healing.'

'Please, Martin, please just give it a try. I couldn't bear to lose Jacob – it would break my heart.'

My mind was already made up and, after hastily finishing my meal, I told Jennifer that I would be back later and followed Julie and her family to their car.

We arrived at Julie's mother's house and went into the room where the patient was lying stretched out in its basket. The whole family seemed to be present: father, mother, brother, sisters, even Bart and Naomi were there, watching. I took one look at the cat and wondered how on earth I had ended up in such an awkward and highly emotional situation. By this stage the poor animal looked as though it was going through its final death throes; its eyes were rolling from side to side and spasms shook its entire body. I began to feel a little claustrophobic, with all the family watching me expectantly, so I excused myself and walked through into the back garden for some fresh air. Naomi's brother and Bart followed closely behind me.

'It's not looking too good is it?' said Bart, who always seemed to have a way with words!

Naomi's brother had an even more negative outlook. 'I'd give that poor beast only a two per cent chance of making it through the night.'

I couldn't exactly put my finger on it, but that last statement had an immediate and profound effect on me. 'Nonsense, that beast, as you so charmingly put it, will survive – of that I am sure.'

I asked the family for a little privacy, then began to pray as hard as I could for the healing energy to stream through my arms, immediately laying my hands on the tortured animal. The response was almost immediate: the eyes stopped rolling and the spasms became less frequent. After 20 minutes I'd finished and the cat lay peacefully in its basket.

The family thanked me for coming to the cat's aid and promised to inform me about its progress.

I told Jennifer about the episode, and warned her that I didn't hold out much hope for the cat.

'You've done your best,' she said.

If only this incident had occurred later on in the *Magnetiseren* course, I thought, at least then I'd have had some idea how to approach and even handle such a situation successfully. Oh well, I consoled myself, it's now in the lap of the gods!

Monday came and went without the expected telephone call, which led me to believe that the cat had, after all, died and because of the family's grief, they had forgotten to telephone me. Late on Tuesday evening, when I'd completely given up hope, Julie telephoned, full of joy and happiness. The cat had made a full recovery and was playing around as if nothing had happened. Julie thanked me for my help and promised to return the favour one day.

A tremendous feeling of relief and wonderment came over me. I had, once again, and despite my own self doubt, proved to myself that miracles could happen, given the right set of circumstances and a little more self belief. Oh ye of little faith, I thought, bathed in a warm glow of satisfaction.

Wednesday evening's Psychometry readings started disappointingly. The group had all swapped photographs and then, following Ian's instructions, we held the photograph in our hands, closed our eyes and tried to isolate out any impressions we received.

Three of the group had already had their turn and demonstrated varying degrees of accuracy with their impressions. Now it was my turn.

I couldn't see or feel a thing until, full of disappointment, I opened my eyes and looked at the stranger who stared at me from the photograph. Almost immediately an aura appeared around her body and impressions began to flood into my mind.

I described in great detail the pictures I was seeing, despite their obviously emotional content. I saw and felt the pain experienced by this particular woman during childbirth, and was able to add that she also had problems with her reproductive organs.

By this time, the whole class had fallen completely silent.

Ian asked me to hand him the photograph and after careful study announced that he could only find a small emotional problem, located in the throat area. The girl who had brought the photograph, could neither confirm nor deny any of the statements. The photograph belonged to a sceptical work colleague of hers, and she promised to check the information with her colleague and inform the group in the following lesson.

The following week, I had almost forgotten the incident with the photograph and had just arrived at Ian's farmhouse, when the girl came running in after me.

'Martin, Martin,' she said breathlessly. 'Everything you said last week was absolutely spot on. My colleague would like to meet you for a reading, if that's all right with you?'

I refused politely, explaining that I didn't feel ready for such readings. The girl's colleague had always been sceptical about such matters, especially after having visited one or two so-called psychics for what turned out to be 'a load of nonsense'. That is, until she'd heard what I'd said. The girl told the rest of the group about my success and Ian congratulated me.

I felt rather awkward. After all, Ian was the learned one, not me, and the last thing I wanted was any sort of competition to develop between us.

At the end of the lesson, Ian called me over and invited me to his house the following afternoon. He said that the other members of the school staff would be present and I could undergo a four in one *Magnetiseren* massage. I accepted his invitation, wondering if Tom would come up with any other psychic information concerning myself.

The next afternoon Tom, Ian and myself made our way into Ian's treatment room, whose walls were lined with all manner of spiritual books and pictures.

'Before we begin,' said Ian, 'will you have a look at this photograph, Martin, and tell me what you see?'

Ian has invited me here to show me up in front of Tom, I thought. Well, let us see. I stared at the photograph of an attractive brown-haired girl until, sure enough, the faint outline of a coloured aura began to appear.

'This person is someone very close to you, Ian,' I began hesitantly. 'I get the distinct impression that although she was born in Holland she doesn't live here any more and she is quite depressed concerning a relationship.' I paused for breath, then filled in a few other details. After I'd finished, Ian and Tom stared at each other in amazement.

'What's the matter? Have I said something wrong?'

'No, not at all,' began Ian. 'You have just given me an accurate description of my daughter's life.'

'This can't be true,' I stammered, totally bewildered. 'I just used what came into my mind, nothing else.'

'Well, I knew I was right about you,' said Tom, beaming from ear to ear.

The afternoon ended with a *Magnetiseren* massage for me, and another ten thousand questions!

TEN

One thing I'd learnt about Holland since living there was that the people love to gossip. The Dutch grapevine seemed to me to be more intricate and more successful than any of the media channels, and before I knew it I had started to receive a steady stream of telephone calls from people who had 'heard about' me.

Slowly but surely Jennifer's prophetic statement was becoming reality and I ended up seeing people from all walks of life, mainly during the evening. Conversation would lead, inevitably, to the person's 'problem', which they hoped I could solve. I did my best, and sent them away. After a short period, I would receive an excited telephone call, full of praise and thanks for what I had achieved. In the end, I wished that one, just one, of the problems wouldn't be solved within the allotted time period.

Finally, it seemed that my wish had been granted. I had at last failed to deliver. I felt completely exhausted but more than a little relieved, especially as the great burden of responsibility seemed to be lifted from my shoulders.

I decided then to stop using that particular gift of mine. Meanwhile I'd received a set of tarot cards as a present and, purely on an experimental basis, I began to give readings. I did it first of all for friends and then for many of the other people who were still visiting me for readings in the evenings. However, this intense period of readings also began to take its toll, especially since some of the sessions were so successful that they sometimes lasted three hours or more.

Following a much needed period of recuperation during the Christmas festivities of 1994, I decided to limit the readings to perhaps one or two people per month, in an effort to avoid burning myself out, both physically and mentally.

The relief was overwhelming. I felt that an extremely stressful and exciting chapter of my life had ended, although I was sure that there would be more surprises to come. Not for a while, I thought. I need to get back down to earth and try to return to some kind of normality.

Any ideas I had about returning to normality were soon to be shattered.

The first few days of 1995 had passed peacefully enough, until I received a telephone call from Julie. She had fallen in love with one of her old flames, and they planned to marry.

'Congratulations, I'm very pleased for you. When's the date?' I said enthusiastically.

'That's the problem,' she began, setting intuitive alarm bells ringing in my mind. 'We want to live together first, to make sure we're compatible.'

'What's wrong with that?'

'Well, Harry, my boyfriend, has been trying to sell his house since last October without success, and I just wondered if you wouldn't mind helping out.'

My heart sank. For the second time in my life I'd tried to distance myself from the paranormal world and once again fate had intervened.

I tried to put Julie off the idea, by telling her about my previous failures, to no avail, and in the end I agreed to meet Julie and Harry at my house the following evening. Apparently it had taken her almost three weeks to convince the sceptical Harry to give me this chance.

Sunday evening arrived sooner than I'd anticipated. The coffee had just been set, the biscuits neatly placed, Dutch style, on our white-tiled coffee table, when the doorbell signalled the premature arrival of Julie and Harry.

Jennifer volunteered to answer the door and welcome our guests, while I sought out a suitable New Age CD, to add a little extra ambience to the occasion.

The evening turned out well in the end. I was surprised at Harry's friendly and open manner, as I'd built up a picture of a disbelieving and quite sceptical person, after listening to Julie's description of him over the telephone. Which just goes to show that you must never pre-judge a person, no matter what the circumstances.

During the course of the evening, I made up my mind. I would do my best to help Harry to sell his house. After explaining my method of meditation, I asked him to remain as open-minded as possible on the subject, and I gave them a time limit of one month from the present, adding that if it was going to work the first positive signs should manifest themselves within a week or two.

At the end of the evening Julie and Harry embarrassed me by presenting me with a music token for my time and effort. I thanked them and as I was showing them to the front door, Julie promised to contact me if anything turned up.

Jennifer had already begun to clear away the evening's debris, but declined my offer of help.

'You'd better go and do your meditation before you forget!' she teased, knowing full well how uncomfortable I was at the prospect of being drawn once again into the stressful world of 'miracles'.

I trudged dejectedly up the antique spiral staircase, heading towards the reading room, where I would select a meditation cassette and light a stick of incense, in preparation for my 30 minutes of deep and tranquil contemplation.

Thoughts of trying to succeed where estate agents had failed weighed heavily on my mind. According to Harry, there had been just one enquiry in four months. According to the estate agent the asking price was too high, while Harry couldn't afford to lower it, or he would be caught in the negative equity trap.

'How did it go?' asked Jennifer as she got ready for bed.

'We'll just have to wait and see,' I replied, as nonchalantly as possible, though without any real conviction. After all, it had been several months since my last attempt, and that had ended in a disappointing failure.

Three days later, on Wednesday afternoon, I decided to visit one of the art and craft shops in Hoorn. I wanted to buy some canvas and oil paints and try and channel my overflowing creativity into painting, which was one of my favourite hobbies. I bought the equipment I needed and made my way towards home, clutching a bagful of goodies. My mind was filled with a series of weird and wonderful heavenlike landscapes, ready for an afternoon of self-indulgence.

I had almost reached home when I heard someone calling my name. I turned around to see Harry and Julie walking quickly towards me. What on earth are they doing in Hoorn? I thought, remembering that they lived in a village some distance away. Harry threw both of his arms around me in a rough bear-hug, shouting at the top of his voice, 'Brilliant, brilliant,' much to the surprise of the other shoppers.

'What! What's happened?' I managed to stammer as Harry let me go and then took my hand, shaking it heartily.

'Listen,' he began excitedly. 'I don't know what you did, but whatever it was, it worked!' He then went on to explain that since their visit to me five different parties had suddenly, 'out of the blue', wanted to buy his house for the set asking price. Following speedy negotiations with his estate agent in Hoorn, a contract had been signed that very day. 'It's nothing short of a miracle,' he said enthusiastically and he swore that never again would he be sceptical about my powers. I congratulated them both, and they promised to send us an invitation to their wedding later on in the year.

I reached home in a state of shock and spent the rest of the afternoon in a semi-conscious trance, trying to come to terms with what had happened, striving to keep my somewhat slippery grip on reality.

During the months that followed, aided by many a prayer and meditation, my life began to return to what I considered to be normal. The evening readings had slowly but surely come to an end, allowing me a long-overdue period of abstinence from spiritual matters, and giving me time and space to consider my future.

Throughout this whole turbulent period of discovery, my friend Mary had determined to further her education. However, we met almost monthly, visiting each other when time and circumstances allowed.

After a particularly lengthy and interesting discussion, I went to make us both a refreshing drink and Mary decided to check the latest concert information on the television. While she flicked through a selection of European channels, I heard a sound that sent shivers up and down my spine.

She knew intuitively that something was the matter. I asked her to turn the channels back, two or three stations. She did so, and there it was. Yet again, documentary films and newsreel footage from the Second World War, showing crews of Bomber Command, preparing for a night-bombing raid over Germany.

I stood listening to the drone of the bombers as they took off, my mind filling again with those nagging pictures I'd recalled under regression therapy, which sent shivers of uncontrollable and unrecognizable emotions through my entire body.

After a rather emotional discussion, Mary asked if I would accompany her to the local library. 'The fresh air will do you good,' she said as we set off past the harbour, towards the library.

Once inside, she began to search through the varied magazine section, in the aptly named Reading Cafe. This was a section of the library that I'd overlooked when I was searching for books about RAF Bomber Command, shortly after my regression. Anyway, I thought, while waiting somewhat impatiently for Mary, this particular section has magazines and newspapers only.

Mary found what she had been looking for and we were about to leave, when I spotted a collectors' magazine, on the front of which were the words, 'Mini-special about the Second World War and its collectable items'. I asked Mary to wait for a moment while I flipped the pages to the item about the war.

The article was written by a Dutchman from the south of Holland. His interest was in collecting and collating information about the aircraft of all types and nationalities that had been shot down in the area between Holland, Belgium and Germany. His name and address were given at the end of the article. I asked Mary what she thought about the idea of writing a letter to the man. She pointed out that I had nothing to lose so I made a note of his name and address, said goodbye to Mary and hurried home to write my letter of enquiry. Somewhere in the back of my mind, though, I knew that the aircraft I'd seen while in regression was not shot down over the south of Holland; it was definitely somewhere in the north.

Six days later I received a rather disappointing, though not unexpected, letter, in which my correspondent explained that my information was rather scanty and, although he had searched his computer files thoroughly, he could find no trace at all of Richard Seymour. He added that he had sent a copy of my letter to one of his colleagues, who researched and collected information about the RAF losses over Holland. Well, I thought, nothing ventured, nothing gained; that's probably the last I'll hear about that.

During the weeks that followed I tried my best to avoid watching the television. The celebrations of the fiftieth anniversary of the ending of the War in Europe seemed to be the subject of either films or documentaries on nearly every European television station.

I found it difficult to come to terms with the strange emotional feelings that I associated with the pictures and decided to ignore television entirely. I even began to question my motives in writing to the collector in the first place. Why, I thought, why had I bothered, knowing full well that reincarnation is for me a fact, a deeply anchored and rooted fact, that was only reinforced by the memories recalled whilst under hypnosis? The only possible reason for my sudden and instinctive urgent desire to find factual evidence about Richard Seymour and the manner in which he had died was that I felt that I was being manipulated, in some strange way, in order to provide scientifically sound proof that reincarnation occurs.

Why me? I thought, on more than a number of occasions. I certainly didn't require this final and unequivocal proof; after all, I'd been party to all manner of spiritual discoveries and truths during my relatively short life, and had just about managed to retain my sanity.

My day of reckoning arrived some two weeks after my first letter from the collector. Jennifer and I were enjoying our first cup of coffee of that Saturday morning. I was seated on the settee as Jennifer went downstairs to collect our post.

'There's one for you,' she called, as she came back up the stairs. 'Who do you know from south Holland?' Another disappointment, I thought, realizing that it must be from the collector's colleague. But nothing on earth could have prepared me for the following few minutes.

I opened the letter, and there it was, in the shape of a Second World War crash report. It confirmed everything I'd seen whilst under hypnosis – the time and date of the crash, the area of north Holland, Richard Seymour's age and the fact that he was a wireless operator. It even confirmed that he was listed as missing, which fitted in perfectly with the information I'd recalled about that last, fatal bombing mission. Last but not least, in the top right-hand corner of the report was a photocopy of his epitaph, which confirmed that his father was a vicar.

I sat staring at the report in my hand, wondering if this whole charade was merely a vivid daydream, while simultaneously recalling the catalogue of coincidences that had finally led me to this almost holy moment of spiritual revelation.

For the first and probably last time in my life my mind seemed to explode into a myriad of brightly coloured stars, each one containing the secrets of the universe, which were so simple in their construction that they defied logic.

I gazed into eternity, to the creation of time itself, and our tiny universe paled into obscurity when compared to the far greater and more complex universes which, though invisible to the human eye, run parallel to our own.

All but one or two of the wondrous planets were inhabited by spiritual beings who, it seemed, had the ability to penetrate the veils of time that separated our different worlds, in order to materialize on Earth. Their task was to impart information about our own development here on Earth.

My few moments of spiritual enlightenment were completed when the realization slowly dawned that all this information, including that of creation itself, is stored in each and every one of us. It is waiting for that one special moment in our development when we can open our human consciousness to accept and finally understand the reason for our own existence, which is Love . . . Not an earthly physical love, but a spiritual love and understanding which transcends our human understanding. A love which encapsulates every thing and every being ever created, from the beginning of time, to the never-ending reaches of eternity.

I finally handed the crash report to Jennifer, in complete silence, as I contemplated the love, care and attention that must have guided my spiritual journey on earth so far. I hoped that one day I would be able to repay this divine trust in me . . .

During the period that followed my final proof, I was living on cloud nine, especially after receiving such convincing con-firmation. The only question in my mind was, what next?

After careful consideration I decided to contact a freelance researcher in England, with a view to finding out more about Richard Seymour. This task was made much easier because of the information provided by the crash report, including Richard's squadron and service number. The RAF veteran whose address was given in the freelance research list provided by the Public Record Office agreed to visit the Record Office and obtain as much detail as possible regarding Richard's service in the RAF. He also advised me to write to the Air History Branch of the Ministry of Defence. Two weeks later I received further confirmation that I was still on the right track.

I eagerly ripped open the reply from the Air History Branch and began to read about the history of Richard's squadron. Glancing through the letter my eyes were drawn to the second photocopied page. There it was, a photograph of a Halifax bomber complete with the inscription 'Friday the 13th'. This particular aircraft had been named after the date it had been delivered to the squadron. The familiar warm feeling of *déjà vu* began to envelop my whole being, as my mind tried in vain to reconcile itself with yet another coincidence: Martin Heald, born Friday the 13th 1962.

'How much more proof do you want?' demanded my intuition, shattering any last vestiges of scepticism I'd tried to retain concerning reincarnation.

A few months later, after my euphoria had died down, I made up my mind to go public with the information. My friends were enthusiastic about my story and Jennifer, of course, gave me her wholehearted support. In the end I decided that the best method of bringing my story to the greatest number of people would be to write a book about it, although of course that was easier said than done.

I had never written more than the usual school essay and I didn't even know where to start. Yes, my life so far had been quite eventful enough to justify a book, but something was missing.

Ever since my drowning incident all those years ago, I'd been having the occasional flashback. The memory of that waiting room, coupled with the unforgettable peace and love had always haunted me and I longed to be back there on many occasions. As I got older the flashbacks seemed to grow in intensity. The most active period had been during my schooldays, especially when being taught science-based subjects. The teacher would begin his explanation of one or another of our earthly physical laws and then present the scientific evidence to prove it. My frustration then seemed to know no bounds, I could not disprove these theories although I knew in my heart of hearts that they were not the absolute truth.

Following my regression therapy I tried one of the meditation exercises, in an effort to access those memories. My hypnosis session ended with Richard's death, at the moment when one bright light had arrived to transport him to his next destination, the spiritual realms.

It *must* be possible, I thought, as the meditation tape began. Thirty minutes later I lay on the bed feeling extremely frustrated. I had reached the same level of trance as in my hypnosis session, and I had relived those last few moments of Richard's life, but I was being prevented from going any further than the light. I tried on numerous other occasions without getting any further and decided in the end that if and when the time were ripe I would be allowed access to those 'hidden' memories.

After two weeks of meditation I'd still not managed to break through the spiritual veil that separated the death of Richard from my own birth. After one particularly frustrating morning of meditation, I came to the conclusion that I wasn't going to be given access to the spiritual realms no matter how hard I tried. Well, that's the end of my book, I thought, as I stared at the bedroom ceiling before closing my eyes and drifting off into a deep sleep.

I'd been asleep for perhaps an hour when I heard a deep male voice calling my name. I tried to open my eyes to see who it was but my eyelids refused to budge. The next moment I felt myself rising out of my physical body, and in one movement found myself standing outside the entrance to a cave, in front of a Tibetan monk.

'Hello Martin,' said this strangely familiar man.

'Who are you, and what am I doing here?' I ventured.

'My name is John. I am one of your spiritual guides,' he replied and began to explain that we'd met hundreds of times in the past and that he had been in constant contact with me over countless differing incarnations. 'I know you must be confused, Martin, but cast your mind back to a few of the so-called coincidences and discoveries in your life.'

I had just started to do this when John interrupted me. 'Think

back to the occasion when you'd given up a job against all your
better judgement and, full of desperation, you suddenly remembered a book you'd been given concerning meditation for your
28th birthday and decided to try out one of the meditations.'

A tremendous feeling of love and understanding coursed
through my soul as I recalled my previous meeting with John.
He began to explain that he would 'channel' the information
regarding my missing time spent in the spiritual realms.

'All you have to do is completely relax before you begin to
write and I will do the rest, but you must remember to write
everything that comes into your mind, no matter how far fetched
and unreal it may seem.'

John's words echoed around my bedroom as I awoke with
a start. I didn't for one moment have any doubt as to the reality
of my experience and after excitedly relaying the day's events
to Jennifer decided to make a start on my book the very
next morning.

ELEVEN

The by now familiar images of Richard's untimely death were still deeply etched in my mind as I began to relive the events following his/my violent end. Then my feelings turned to joy at the prospect of meeting my friends and soulmates from incarnations past.

Within a short space of time I seemed to forget even the very existence of the planet Earth, with all its trials and tribulations – here, there was so much to do, so many people to meet and so much to learn.

I'd been recovering from my traumatic death for two or three days, when an extremely beautiful female came briskly into my room.

'Come on, Richard, it's time you were out and about,' she chided me.

I lay there on the bed, completely transfixed by this angelic presence who stood before me, dressed in a soft pale blue and white silky robe. Her blond almost transparent hair was carefully tied into a ponytail.

'My name's Juliette,' she introduced herself, helping me off the bed. 'Are you still feeling quite heavy?'

'Yes,' I replied, staring into her sparkling emerald-green eyes.

'Don't worry, after a refreshing walk you'll feel completely energized.'

I followed Juliette down a corridor, until we stepped outside. The view that greeted me was breathtaking, with lush green hills and mountains as far as I could see. I stood rooted to the spot, trying to come to terms with this awe-inspiring panorama. I couldn't remember ever having seen such a colourful and evocative landscape on Earth. The sky seemed twenty times more bright and contained an almost unlimited number of blue- and green-tinted hues, blending in perfectly with the distant turquoise mountain ranges.

Juliette's voice shook me out of my reverie. 'Come on, there's plenty more to see.'

As we strolled slowly towards the nearest mountain, Juliette explained that it was her task to show some of the new arrivals around the area, as a sort of first orientation. I was just about to question her when I caught sight of the most marvellous waterfall I had ever seen, cascading down the mountain from high above us, rippling and sparkling down the hill, finally culminating in a crystal-clear river we could see just ahead of us.

We made our way to the river bank and sat down to watch this magnificent spectacle. I noticed an amazing variety of flowers and other plants, and drank in their heady aroma. Each blade of grass seemed delicate and clear, seemingly created with its own special purpose.

'Well,' prompted Juliette. 'What do you think?'

'It must have taken years of careful cultivation to create such beauty,' I replied, looking around me.

'Thank you,' she said, smiling.

'What do you mean?'

'Well, I'd heard that you enjoyed the countryside whilst you were on Earth, so I created this for you, whilst you were recovering.'

'*You* created all this!' I replied, completely dumbfounded.

'Yes, but don't worry, you will soon be able to create your own landscape.'

I was lost in thought, during the short walk back. Juliette explained that a new course of lessons would be starting shortly and advised me to attend, adding that it could only be to my own advantage. She pointed towards an imposing looking building, almost directly opposite the entrance to the recovery block, which she said was the classroom.

'Are you coming in?' I asked her, outside the doorway. She apologized, explaining that she was going to see her parents. I thanked her for her company and asked if I would see her again.

'You never know,' she replied, as I made my way through into the corridor of the recovery block. I turned round to wave her goodbye and was astonished to see that she had already gone. How strange I thought to myself, arriving back in my room, not even a good-bye. I lay down on the bed feeling fully refreshed, although my mind was full of unanswered questions.

I must have fallen asleep, although I cannot remember dreaming, until Juliette's voice interrupted my slumber.

'Richard, it's time you were moving. The lessons are about to begin!'

I looked around the room, fully expecting to see Juliette standing over me. She was nowhere to be seen.

'You'll soon get used to this sort of communication,' she added, laughing.

I made my way over to the classroom and was surprised to see other people, already seated. I took my place, glancing at my fellow pupils. There seemed to be a mixture of races and creeds, from many differing cultures and backgrounds. I noticed an absence of school desks and exercise books. The chairs were arranged in a semi-circle, not in uniform rows. Well, there's definitely no lack of inspiration in this classroom, I thought, as I gazed out of the windows which ran along three sides of the room, allowing the pupils a completely uninterrupted view of the breathtaking panorama.

Suddenly the teacher entered the room and introduced himself. What a strange sight, I thought, staring at his violet-coloured toga, held together with a bright orange cord. After a few words of introduction, the teacher began to explain the forgotten laws and methods of creation. The faculty was available to every one of Earth's inhabitants, although the interval between thought and manifestation on Earth was so long that the human mind failed to see the connection between fantasy and reality. We therefore failed to make use of one of the most powerful natural laws of the universe.

'In your present spirit form,' he went on, 'you can create anything your heart desires. It's just a question of imagination and practice.'

No sooner had he uttered the words than his toga began to change colour and within the space of a few seconds it had assumed every colour imaginable until finally returning to its original violet hue.

A tangible buzz of excitement engulfed the classroom as the teacher described some of the earthly examples of this particular form of creation. For example, one of our fellow pupils, Haseem, had been born into an extremely poor Indian family and had spent his childhood begging on the streets to help feed his family. Every night before he went to sleep he would daydream about having enough money to be able to go to school and educate himself, enabling him to move up in society and there-fore clothe and feed his family. Haseem had almost given in to his fate when his daydream became reality. He had spent the best part of a morning begging to no avail, when he was approached by a kind looking foreigner who, without any hint of an introduction, offered him a live-in position as a cleaner. Of course, Haseem gratefully accepted this unexpected opportunity and within the space of a few years the family's fortunes had undergone a complete change, although at the time Haseem hadn't given his daydreaming a second thought.

'Don't forget,' added our teacher, 'when you are reborn on the Earth you are taught from a very early age earthly laws and lessons of earthly life, which most of you will adhere to as part of your spiritual learning. But as the individual soul progresses so too will awareness increase until the earthly and spiritual realms become so closely intertwined, that the need to reincarnate becomes obsolete.'

The actual method of travelling seemed so simple in theory. All one had to do was to visualize a person or destination, with enough strength, and within an instant you were there with the person or in the place. I soon began to master the technique after a few initial embarrassing mistakes, arriving completely unannounced, in all manner of places and situations. What a novel way to travel, I thought at first, until I noticed that more and more people were actually walking. The realization struck me – here I was, travelling around this magnificent place in the blink of an eyelid, without ever slowing down or stopping to appreciate some of this breathtaking scenery.

After what I estimated to be about five Earth years of rest and recuperation, I was told of a course of lessons which might be of use to me in my next incarnation. Nobody was forced into attending any lessons, but I felt that these were important and that I should learn everything I could. It would help me if I had to return to Earth once again.

One lesson that seemed especially important concerned the human aura and its special function, not only as a protection mechanism, but also as an early-warning system for sickness, both mental and physical. We were allowed a brief glimpse of the future, showing aura-photography equipment being installed in hospitals as well as in doctors' surgeries. This enabled people to have two or three check-ups a year, without the danger of over-exposure to X-rays. As a result of these photographs, a potential illness could be eradicated by highly skilled spiritual healers, who would make use of meditation techniques and the trans-ferral of universal light energy to cleanse a patient's aura of any impurities long before their manifestation in the body.

We were also shown how meditation could strengthen the human energy field, if used with the correct combination of food and exercise.

The faculty of human creation belongs to, and is encapsulated within the aura. Using a certain meditation and a strong visualization, the energy field becomes energized and brings into creation the given thought. On Earth the process takes a little while, the exact time depending upon the spiritual depth of the person in question. For some of the more spiritually advanced people on Earth the time between thought and creation is almost instantaneous. Most souls of these types had volunteered to return to Earth. Leading a mostly frugal and nomadic existence, such individuals seemed to turn up in remote mountain settlements at just the right moment, usually during times of extreme hardship, and remaining long enough to impart some of their valuable knowledge. As suddenly as they had arrived they would disappear. The inhabitants would soon forget their mysterious visitor, especially once their crops began to flourish again, just as the stranger had promised. The biblical story of Jesus turning water into wine and the dividing of loaves and fishes, whilst seen as a fable by many people on Earth, now assumed a very factual aspect.

The transference of universal energy from one being to another, with its accompanying healing effect, was apparently still treated as miraculous, or at least as coincidence. I found this particularly sad, because each and every one of us possesses the ability to heal not only ourselves but also our fellow human beings. If only we would remain open, to receive this universal energy!

The lessons we received contained many practical situations and suggestions. Each of us, in turn, would sit in the middle of the group and concentrate upon a sad event or occasion from our previous life, until our emotions closely matched the earthly ones of sadness and depression. The rest of the group would then send a constant stream of healing energy to the subject, who would then feel the energy entering their spiritual body from above, slowly moving downwards until their entire being was filled from top to bottom with uplifting energies, which gave the subject an immediate insight into the reasons behind the original sad event. Individual experiences and continual interaction formed the basis of our lessons, although I found that the most exciting aspect for me was our visit to the library. Our teacher, still wearing his violet toga, had told us how to get there, bade us farewell and presently left the classroom. Following Michael's instructions, we then concentrated on his eloquent description of the library and its surroundings.

The next moment I found myself in the most breathtaking and beautiful garden I could ever have imagined. There, in the distance, stood what could only be described as an architectural miracle. The library itself seemed an exact replica of the buildings I'd seen while reading a book about Greek mythology at school. Filled with excitement and awe, I decided to walk to the library, down the tree-lined grassy pathway, which was bordered on both sides with delightful arrangements of exotic plants and flowers, most of them bearing berries and fruits of such a varied assortment that I couldn't even begin to describe them. A gentle breeze blew, which added yet another element to this wonderful experience – the fragrance of the flowers.

As I approached the marble staircase I could see the rest of the class standing in a group, debating the finer details of this truly marvellous building.

'Come on, Richard, we've been waiting for you,' called James, a former navigator in the RAF, who had died when the landing gear on his aircraft had failed.

'You can't order me about up here,' I replied, laughing.

'Sorry, old chap, I'd forgotten,' grinned James, amused by the irony of the situation.

After negotiating the highly polished steps, we entered the library. It was filled with the hustle and bustle normally associated with a market place and I couldn't see any sign of any bookshelves, let alone books! I excused myself from the rest of the group, and decided to explore the vast interior of this 'library'.

After wandering through a seemingly endless maze of corridors and hallways, without seeing the slightest hint of a book, I began to wonder if our teacher had played some kind of joke on us. I was just about to leave the building, when I spotted Michael walking towards me.

'Ah, there you are, Richard. Any luck yet?'

'Well, actually no,' I replied, somewhat embarrassed. 'I don't seem to be able to find any books.'

He began to laugh. 'It's always the same with newcomers.'

'What do you mean?'

'Haven't you noticed that most of the doors are marked with different letters of the alphabet?'

'Yes.'

'Well, whatever subject you find interesting, archaeology for example, all you have to do is enter one of the rooms with the letter "A" and the rest will become apparent.'

I thanked Michael for his advice and set off once again, hopefully a little wiser. I determined to enter the first door I came across, whatever letter it might be.

'T', that will do, I thought, walking into a dazzlingly bright, almost electrically charged and perfectly circular room. That's strange, no windows. Where's the light coming from?

My question remained unanswered, as I sat down on an extremely comfortable padded floor, wondering which subject to choose. Travel, that will do. I've always been interested in travelling. I began to concentrate on aircraft and within an instant the whole atmosphere of the room had changed. Moments later I'd relived and watched man's first attempt at flight, right through the astonishing history of aviation and well into the future, although I found it difficult to believe what most of the future newsreel was showing. There was a passenger aircraft with a cone-shaped front that could fly faster than a bullet, and a so-called 'space shuttle', that could transport people to outer space and back again.

Further revelation about future travel followed quickly, including cars that could run on solar batteries, small motor-cycles that flew high above the ground, fuelled by compressed air, and trains that seemed to be floating above a single track, by way of 'electro-magnetism'.

After visiting one or two of the other rooms, I decided to make my way home. In Earth terms the nearest description of this library would be as a sort of A to Z of the universe, expanding day by day, stretching out into eternity as the never-ending quest of creation continues.

By this time, I'd become quite skilled in the field of creation. I tapped my seemingly endless enthusiasm and knowledge to create my own little dream home. I surrounded myself on all sides with the most breathtaking landscape I could imagine. There were green mountains and foothills, complete with running streams and springs of crystal-clear water, all of which culminated in a fantastic series of cascades at the bottom of my new garden. The flora I had created was in hues limited only by the bounds of my ever-expanding imagination.

Food and sleep had absolutely no parallel with the Earth. I was constantly absorbing energy either from the streams of water or from the light, which shone continuously. It was possible to eat the vegetation, which grew in abundance, but once I had adapted to my spiritual body, there was no need. This body seemed to be a perfect replica of my earthly one, apart from the fact that I was completely weightless. There was no possibility of concealing emotion of any sort, as the corresponding change in the colours of energy was reflected instantly in the aura which surrounded each individual.

Sleep soon became a thing of the past, thanks to the continual stream of energy, although after an intensive period of learning, it was advisable to rest for a short time.

Eventually I decided to join the art classes, and soon became quite adept at both landscape scenes and abstract work. It soon became clear to me that many of the famous artists upon Earth had used their skills both consciously and unconsciously to open the human mind to spirituality through their creativity. Time and time again our teacher reminded us that while on Earth our creativity was limited only by our fantasy, and adding that the seeds that were sown during our lessons here would eventually come to fruition, depending upon our own individual actions and deeds.

It was during one of these classes that I met Jen. I suppose you could call it love at first sight. She was such a beautiful girl that I couldn't stop looking at her. From the first time that our eyes met across the art room I was completely smitten by her. She had deeply hypnotic hazel-brown eyes which seemed to draw me in towards her. Finally I couldn't stand it any longer, and turned away to continue my work of art . . .

At the end of the lesson Jen walked over to me and, after a rather shy introduction, invited me to a concert to be given by the students of an experimental music academy. After accepting her invitation, Jen and I arranged to meet at my house when the time came.

For once, time really started to drag by until Jen arrived. She asked me if I'd ever been to one of these concerts before. I explained my lack of real interest in music.

'You'll enjoy this one,' she told me, and began to explain that the instruments were newly developed and purely experimental. If they should prove to be a success they would eventually be re-invented upon Earth, after undergoing a short trial period. Needless to say, I could not wait to arrive at the concert building.

We held hands and in a split second we had arrived outside what looked like a gigantic cathedral. The enormous size of this structure took me completely by surprise. Definitely an architectural nightmare, I thought, though I did admire the central dome, which looked as though it had been constructed from one enormous piece of shiny black obsidian, in which was embedded a glittering array of stars.

The scene that greeted us inside surpassed my wildest dreams. The electric atmosphere, coupled with an intense feeling of anticipation, was almost too much to bear. As Jen and I made our way through the throng of thousands of excited souls, I managed to catch a quick glimpse of the musicians and their instruments, already set up on the stage.

'Looks to me like an ordinary piano concerto,' I remarked to Jen, who had by this time found our places high above the stage, although I had to admit that I'd never seen such tiny pianos before.

We'd just taken our seats when the conductor walked on to the stage to take his place on a small raised podium, in front of the musicians. Immediately, he began to conduct the orchestra. The whole building filled with the most beguiling music I had ever heard, which was also combined with colour. I could feel every note and its corresponding colour resonating deep within my very being. Within a few minutes the audience became an integral part of the orchestra. Musicians and audience intermingled and combined perfectly, to produce one great soul of music and colour.

The end of this exhilarating concert came only too soon. I turned around to see the audience's reaction. Every member of the audience had somehow integrated the colours and music within their soul. The whole building shone brilliantly from top to bottom. I felt completely overwhelmed, while at the same time I experienced a feeling of total harmony, peace and love which would, I felt, stay with me forever.

At the end of this particularly enjoyable and exciting first day together, Jen informed me that our meeting in the art class wasn't a coincidence and that we were meant to be together again. This took me completely by surprise, as I had put our encounter down to chance. I asked her what she meant.

'I will come to see you again shortly, and take you to the great library,' she said, adding, 'then, and only then, will you be able to fully understand how and why some of these "coincidental" meetings take place.'

TWELVE

The next few days were spent deep in thought, trying to figure out what Jen had meant. After a while my thoughts turned to that great concert. I had a burning desire to find out more about these inventors and their 'special' inventions.

Following a period of rest and meditation, I concentrated on the musicians. Within an instant I was transported to a small town, surrounded by picturesque countryside which for the first time included animals that we had on Earth. Cows grazed in the lush meadows, horses ran wild, squirrels in the trees, rabbits in the fields, and sheep with young lambs to name but a few. I decided to walk for once and enjoy this magnificent creation. I was immediately approached by one of the wild horses which communicated with me telepathically. I received its special feelings of love and joy at being able to live in such a wonderful environment, without a hint of stress or illness. This short communication made me see that most animals on Earth have almost the same feelings and emotions as human beings. In that respect they deserve to be treated with the same degree of loving kindness shown to other living beings. I thanked the wonderful creature who, in turn, bowed its head low to the ground, nodded a few times as if in agreement, then quickly and gracefully galloped off towards the rest of the horses.

I continued my journey towards the town and had just reached the first group of buildings when, to my astonishment, a man called my name. For the first time since my arrival, I felt as if I was looking at a very spiritual and holy man. Any thoughts I had had about God or Jesus had simply been forgotten about, until this moment.

This is it, I thought, walking towards the archetypal picture of Jesus – dazzling white robes, silvery-white hair and beard. His intensely blue eyes seemed to look right through me, as he introduced himself as David. He explained, to my secret disappointment, that he had been sent there to meet me.

After making his excuses to the other people, he beckoned me to follow him.

'Come,' he said. 'I have such a lot to show you, in such a short space of time. I hope you realize how privileged you are, to be able to visit our town. Not everyone is given this opportunity,' he continued, smiling at me. I decided immediately to concentrate fully on the experiences which were to follow.

The first building we entered was a gigantic transparent pyramid, which seemed to reach out into infinity. At the top, in the middle of the pyramid, high above what seemed to be a workplace, stood the largest and purest diamond or crystal I had ever seen. I was just about to ask David about this wonderful piece of craftsmanship when he interrupted me. 'Just try to observe, and save any questions until later.'

The sight before me was amazing. Workbenches were arranged in a somewhat haphazard manner, scattered around the inside of the pyramid. Upon each stood a variety of constructions and machinery. I watched in silence as each one of the men in turn took their place directly beneath the magical crystal, assuming a meditational sitting position. Moments later, there followed an exchange of bright, almost blinding, energy between crystal and person. The process was repeated until all the workers had returned to their benches and were working swiftly and confidently, with renewed vigour and purpose.

After a few minutes, David motioned me to follow him and, once outside the pyramid, began immediately to answer my questions.

'The people in the pyramid are spiritually highly advanced, and do not have to reincarnate upon the Earth. They are continually inventing new devices to help mankind on Earth and, as you probably realized, they receive direct inspiration from our Creator, via the crystal.' He paused momentarily, deep in thought.

'When a new device is created up here, it is tried and tested and if it receives the necessary approval, the inventor is then allowed to meet the potential inventor on Earth.'

'This meeting takes place in a land that exists between here and the Earth, mainly during the Earth person's dreams. He or she is then instructed which materials to use in its final construction, together with its best application.'

When I asked David to give me an example, he told me about a device which would bundle the universal light energy into a powerful tool which would, eventually, be used on Earth to cure some of the worst sicknesses and diseases, such as cancer, without harming the human body.

'Light, you see, is divided into many thousands of different frequencies and strengths. In the future, many scientists on Earth will discover this fact and will be able to utilize the various frequencies to destroy completely any internal cancers or sicknesses, without harming any of the vital organs or the human body itself.'

Another device being developed would be ready for introduction just before the end of the present Earth century.

'Many tracts of land will become poisoned in the future, due to large-scale farming technology, leading to a widespread food shortage. This new device will be used to electrically charge the molecules of one of the lesser-known gases on Earth, which would pass through and completely eradicate any impurities within the food, whilst simultaneously adding to its nourishment value.'

We continued our magical journey, heading back towards the countryside. I followed David down a long and winding country lane, bordered on both sides by marvellous plants, fruit and flowers. The scents were almost overpowering. After a further brisk walk, we arrived at our new destination, an area of overgrown jungle, full of strange creatures, insects, exotic plants, huge trees and, by the sound of it, some form of primates.

David repeated his earlier request to observe first, and ask questions later. We continued through the depths of the jungle. A short trek later we came across a large building, a greenhouse in a clearing. David spoke to one of the people inside the building and motioned me to follow.

Once inside, I began to fully appreciate the enormity of this strange construction. I watched intently as one of the workers busied herself with a syringe-type instrument. She walked over to one of several clearly marked tanks, siphoned off an exact amount of translucent liquid and then proceeded to inject it carefully into one of the plants, which were labelled in Latin. She seemed completely oblivious to our presence. David smiled at me and nodded towards the doorway, signalling the end of this particular adventure.

'This place,' he began, 'is a complete replica of a jungle on Earth. The people you saw inside were busy inventing and injecting the plants with new substances and chemicals, all of course produced naturally. By the end of the present Earth century they will be discovered and utilized by enlightened scientists. Their function is prevention and eradication of many diseases, addictions and sicknesses, that were previously thought of as incurable.'

This was almost too much to take in at one go. I asked David if I could remain and rest in this marvellous environment for a while. He agreed and left me alone to try to assimilate all of this new information.

I sat amongst the undergrowth, trying to take everything in. I was surrounded by the most wonderful scents, which seemed to waft around for a while, to be replaced by a completely different, even more pungently sweet odour. Insects were singing in chorus with the constantly changing atmosphere and scents.

David reappeared, startling me momentarily.

'Grasp my hands and close your eyes. This is going to be quite a long journey.'

I paused for a second, wondering what David could possibly mean by 'long journey' as most of the previous journeys had taken place within the blink of an eyelid. I grasped his hands as he had asked and, after two flashes of intensely bright light, we had arrived.

This looks like one of the universities on Earth, I thought, whilst following David through the main entrance. He introduced himself to a man who looked like a typical headmaster. After a brief conversation, I was told that I could visit any of the rooms that I wished and that David would meet me later, back at the entrance.

I began to walk down the corridor, until I noticed a familiar-looking woman approaching. I was convinced that I'd seen her before, although I couldn't for the life of me remember where, or when. Her hair was grey, cut short with a parting. It matched her knee-length prefect-style dress perfectly. She smiled, held out a perfectly-manicured hand and, after introducing herself as Alison, offered to be my guide. I gladly accepted her offer, immediately following her lead on this seemingly impromptu magical mystery tour. She stopped abruptly, outside one of the many classroom doors.

'Here we are,' she said, opening the door. 'You should find this one interesting.'

It seemed to be an almost perfect replica of a school classroom on Earth. I watched in silence, remembering David's earlier requests to observe first, questions later. Twenty model pupils sat behind highly varnished wooden desks, neatly organized into five rows, with four pupils to each row. Suddenly, the next lesson suddenly began . . .

At the front of the class, on the wall, there appeared to be a special three-dimensional screen, showing short fragments of film which were followed immediately by intense discussion amongst the pupils. Then the whole sequence repeated itself. I recognized a rather young-looking Adolf Hitler, making his first attempts to enter politics, and I was shown the mistakes made by the politicians of the time, when they underestimated his growing popularity. The films were continuing as Alison and I left the classroom.

'The pupils are going to reincarnate on Earth several years into the next century, and will eventually become the politicians and world leaders of a New Age. By learning from previous mistakes, they will be able to ensure lasting peace and harmony for the centuries to follow, therefore allowing unhindered spiritual growth and learning, not previously experienced on Earth.'

I didn't really have enough time to mull over the consequences of this, before Alison had ushered me into the classroom next door.

Inside, the set-up was more or less identical, apart from the subject matter. I watched in silent fascination as apocalyptic scenes from Earth began to unfold on the three-dimensional screen – volcanoes erupted, earthquakes shattered buildings and there were all manner of natural disasters. After a short period of discussion amongst the pupils, the next film began. It showed thousands of people from around the world, many from differing cultures, races and backgrounds, all seated, deep in meditation.

The following film both shocked and amazed me. Once again the Earth was shown, this time without the previous upheavals. I could see that a large part of one of the great continents had been submerged under water, and new islands had been formed in its place. The vast barren deserts had been replaced by fantastically verdant landscapes, filled with a growth of vegetation, unlike anything seen before upon the Earth.

Alison explained to me that the pupils in this particular classroom had incarnated many times on Earth, and would in the future become great and highly respected spiritual teachers. They would use their knowledge to help mankind begin to heal and reshape the Earth, the way it was meant to be. By the use of meditation, by the raising of man's consciousness, spiritual as well as physical, the teachers will help to achieve the total integration of all cultures, races, animals and last, but not least, nature . . .

By now I was once again filled with awe and admiration at some of the situations I had been witness to. Alison suggested a period of rest, leading me through another maze of corridors until we finally stepped outside into what I can only describe as the Garden of Eden. I quickly lost count of the many different varieties of plants, of the shades and nuances of colour. This *has* to be the original Garden of Eden, I thought, as I gazed into a pool of green and blue yet crystal-clear water, which, as always, blended in perfectly with the background.

These beautiful sights, sounds and scents relaxed me totally and completely. I sat down on the soft and dewy grass and went into a deep meditation, my consciousness firmly fixed on this truly marvellous creation.

'I knew you'd be impressed,' said Alison softly from her seat beside me. 'These gardens will soon be created naturally on Earth. They will be "discovered' just before the end of the present Earth century, and used as spiritual retreats by many people, who will find in them a source of rich inspiration.'

I was just about to ask a question, when Alison continued.

'I understand how you must be feeling – just try to be a little more patient. You will soon realize who I am, and who some of the other people that you've met during your time here, are.'

Be patient, I thought. I am being shown some of the miracles of the universe, without knowing who these familiar, loving and patient people are, although I was sure that I would eventually find out.

Before I could dwell on these matters any further Alison ushered me into an enormous hall, packed to capacity. I watched in amazement as a discussion began, which resulted in what appeared to be tens of thousands of bundles of light energy being exchanged from person to person, simultaneously and completely in unison. I had never seen such an awesome sight and I was stunned by the sheer speed of the exchanges. Suddenly the intense activity ceased. On the wall facing us, I could see one of the strange three-dimensional screens appearing, this time on a very much larger scale.

The first film showed the planets of the solar system and their effect upon the soul at birth. The conjunction of certain planets and stars exerts such an influence that most of the new soul's life will be governed by the positions of these planets.

The film ended, to be followed immediately by a frenzied few moments of the same remarkable energy exchanges. The second film began. This showed in great detail the relationship between a new soul, its new Earth name, and the precise numbers attributed to each letter of the name, also the exact date of birth, in days, hours, minutes and seconds. Every bit of this information, numerical and alphabetical, seems to have a direct influence upon the individual's incarnation.

The third and final film encompassed the first two, while also introducing the element of free will, which is capable of affecting the final outcome, either positively or negatively. All this information had to be painstakingly computed for every soul reincarnated upon Earth.

My mind was boggling with this information, as I began to realize why there were so many people involved in what appeared to be an impossible task. I suddenly remembered that during my last incarnation I had been given a book on astrology. After studying it carefully I was impressed enough to consult my father on the subject. He was the vicar of a village parish and, after reading the book through with an open mind, he declared: 'Maybe it's true, maybe not, but everyone must search and find their own truths, whatever they may be.'

Alison explained briefly that the people in this particular hall of learning had once been great and well-known mathematicians, astrologers and scientists, who would eventually be able to put their theories into practice, in the complicated field of reincarnation. As we parted, I thanked her for her patience and understanding, while she assured me that we would meet again soon.

I was still thinking about her, when I met David back at the entrance. He could see my confusion and reassured me that I would meet Alison again, sometime in the future.

'Now, do you think that you're up to making your own way back?'

'I think so,' I replied, thanking him for accompanying me on my journey.

'I will see you again shortly, no need to worry,' he assured me.

David's last words were still echoing in my mind as I arrived back at my beautiful home. I had just begun to contemplate the river, when I noticed a more familiar figure approaching. I felt an abundance of energy well up inside me, as I recognized Jen's beautiful face. In all the excitement, I'd almost overlooked our plans to visit the great library. I apologized to Jen as we sat down side by side in the long green grass. I had just started to explain where I'd been, when a strange but extremely pleasant feeling of togetherness and love came over me.

I looked up and stared guiltily into Jen's hazel-brown eyes, realizing that she too had the same feelings. Before I could react she had moved towards me, and from that moment on we knew instinctively what to do.

We were, in an instant, completely intermingled, both our bodies and souls. I became her and she became me. This indescribable feeling of oneness, not only with my soulmate, but with the whole universe, was complete. I could see stars exploding into a myriad of bright colours and shapes. This fantastic moment of truth and love seemed to last forever, until we both regained control of our senses and lay back on the grass, bathed in a universal light of pure gold.

I knew now the true meaning of the word 'love'. It is when two souls come together, completely open with one another, without secrets. There was, I felt, no comparison on Earth to this absolute love.

We rested in the garden for a while, trying to integrate the new energies that were pulsing in our souls. This was followed by a refreshing swim in the crystal-clear river.

We decided that it was time to visit the great library, and by joining hands were transported instantly to a kind of waiting room, full of people.

This doesn't look much like a library to me, I thought, wondering if Jen had made a mistake, and we'd ended up in one of the spiritual hospitals I'd heard about at school. I was just about to ask Jen where we were, when one of the three doors to our right opened. A deep male voice called out my full Earth name. I looked enquiringly at Jen who, smiling enigmatically, motioned me to go through the door. I walked towards the doorway, leaving Jen behind in the waiting room.

The door closed of its own accord and there I stood, on a black and white squared marble floor. Facing me were 12 men dressed in brown robes, looking for all the world like a gathering of monks. They were seated around an enormous polished oak table. One of the monks, who appeared to be the chairman, asked me if I realized why I was here. Curiosity, I thought to myself, beginning to wonder what sort of joke Jen was playing on me.

'Do you realize that your next incarnation upon Earth will be your last?'

'Yes,' I replied, remembering Michael's revelation during one of my earlier lessons and beginning to feel more and more uneasy at the situation I now found myself in.

'There's nothing to fear, Richard. All souls that undertake their last incarnation, visit here. It's a privilege, you see.' Before I could reply the chairman had thanked me for coming adding that Jen would answer any further queries that I might have.

Jen arose instinctively as I reappeared in the waiting room and began to explain to me what we were doing.

'Before a soul's last incarnation on Earth, they may visit this great library. It contains every detail of the soul's being, beginning with its conception, carrying on through to the first and, subsequently, last incarnation on Earth. It includes all names, all dates, all experiences, even all education, without the omission of one single detail.'

I was silent as Jen informed me that it was also her last incarnation and that we were going to meet up once again, on the Earth plane. This last incarnation was to be the final phase of our shared learning experiences on Earth.

I followed her into the enormous library, walking through row upon row of highly stacked and clearly labelled bookshelves until we had reached the reception desk.

'Names, please?' asked the librarian.

'Richard Seymour and Jennifer Lacroix,' I replied, hoping that Jen wouldn't mind.

The librarian consulted a rather large index book. She flipped over the pages, murmuring to herself as she did so until, having found what she was looking for, she scuttled off into a back room. She quickly reappeared with a slip of paper. Smilingly she handed the paper to me. At first glance it contained bookcase numbers for our own personal histories.

We soon located our books and headed towards one of the more private anterooms, to read them.

I was completely taken aback, not only by the many incarnations I'd had, but also the tremendous detail. I was also amazed at the uncanny regularity of the so-called coincidences that cropped up from one life to the next, especially concerning people's first names. It appeared that some souls kept the same Christian name from one incarnation to the next, not only to avoid confusion but to help the soul's twin with recognition if they were to meet up again in a following incarnation.

It seemed as though all my previous lives were inexorably intertwined. Sometimes I seemed to repeat situations and make the same mistakes, at more or less the same age, on the same date and at the same time. I also experienced life from different viewpoints, both male and female, in order to cultivate a better understanding of the differences, strengths and weaknesses of both sexes.

I looked across at Jen, who was deep in thought.

'What's the matter?'

'Come and look at this,' she said sadly.

I looked in the book, and saw Jen and me living on a farm in the French countryside, with a large family of nine children. Our lives seemed to contain the usual ups and downs associated with a large family. In the end I couldn't cope with the sort of life we had built up and decided to move away, without telling Jen.

I hadn't realized at the time how much she loved me until, after some time spent searching for me, she finally gave up. One evening, after making sure the children were asleep, she drowned herself, leaving our nine children to fend for themselves as orphans.

I never returned to the farm, as I had fallen in love with someone else. Our children were eventually adopted by an uncle and aunt, who acted as mother and father to them.

This whole drama took place during the eighteenth century, but for Jen and me, reliving it in the present, it felt very real indeed. After a short period, spent in quiet consolation, we decided to continue reading our own books.

Another intriguing aspect of the universal law is that nothing ever learnt or experienced falls by the wayside. It does not matter whether it was learnt on Earth, or on the spiritual plane. It all seems to be one gigantic learning experience, divided between two planes of existence, until the individual soul receives enlightenment during its last incarnation on Earth.

Going back through my last three or four incarnations, I could see my awareness building up, until my last incarnation. There I was, a child of eight years old, clairvoyantly relaying information to my parents' friends and relatives. I could see the people laughing out aloud, in a vain attempt to hide their growing discomfort and insecurity. 'Richard's fantasizing again,' they would tell my parents. Luckily for me, my parents were quite spiritually advanced and soon began to realize what was happening to me.

It was wonderful to see my parents once again, and I began to realize how much I'd really missed them. I was just reaching the last few pages of the chapter, and realized that I had no desire to relive those last few months of my life. They were, in any case, still deeply etched into my mind. I flipped the remaining pages over until I had reached the last chapter. That's strange, I thought to myself, staring at the completely blank pages, until the realization dawned on me that they were still to be written!

I waited patiently until Jen had finished reading her book. After a short chat about our various experiences we took our books back to the librarian. We were approaching the reception desk when I noticed a strange-looking presence coming towards the librarian. Following a brief conversation, the almost transparent female apparition wandered off into one of the many rows of bookshelves. Intrigued by this strange sight I asked the librarian who the presence was.

'Oh, that's just a medium, asking for information!'

'Is that allowed?' I asked, completely baffled.

'In certain cases, yes, because the information may be used to guide or help the person in question, to make a difficult choice or a decision that may affect the rest of their life.'

I paused, and remembered always wondering how clairvoyants and mediums obtained their extremely accurate information. Obviously not from any evil forces, as I had frequently been led to believe.

We returned our books, and thanked the kind librarian for her assistance. Once outside the building, Jen and I decided to return to my house, mainly to try and digest some of the information we had been privileged to see. After thoroughly discussing, and even laughing at some of the situations we had found ourselves in, Jen admitted to feeling tired and, after arranging to meet me at the next art class, decided to go home to her parents to rest for a while.

THIRTEEN

I lay on the bed until, slowly but surely, I began to drift into a light meditational sleep, interspersed with the visions and memories of lives gone by. Without any warning David's voice interrupted my dreams. I woke to find him standing at the foot of my four-poster bed. He spoke quite calmly.

'I have something important to tell you. It's quite urgent, Richard. Do you remember your own transition, following your death on Earth?'

'Yes.'

'Well, due to the unfortunate circumstances surrounding your sudden death, it was decided to let you rest for a short while, to give you the time to recover from the trauma.'

'Yes, yes, please get to the point, David.'

'OK. Very shortly your father will be making that same journey. I thought that this would be a perfect opportunity, and quite an experience for everyone involved, if you were all present, relatives and friends, to greet him.'

This came as a total shock to me. I hadn't given my father's death any thought. After the initial shock had subsided, however, I became both excited and emotional at the prospect of seeing my father once again.

'Ready, Richard?'

The next moment we had arrived on the outskirts of a small village, set in the most beautiful countryside imaginable. As we entered the village, I noticed that the rows and rows of houses were joined together. The only noticeable separation was a transparent glass tube, which passed from one house through to the next.

'This is the house,' said David, striding through the open doorway.

'Just in time,' said a man dressed in a doctor's white coat. After ushering us in he introduced himself as Will.

'I'm in charge of the operation, and this is my assistant, Anneke,' he said, smiling at the fair-haired woman in the reception area.

David made his excuses and left the building.

'Come on,' said Will. 'Follow me.'

I followed him through a maze of corridors, until we finally arrived at our destination. The first thing I saw in the small and rather dimly lit room, was a group of people. They were sitting on neatly arranged chairs around an empty bed. I recognized one of my grandfathers, and both of my grandmothers who, after a tearful embrace, introduced me to the other people, who were all friends of my parents.

By now the atmosphere of expectation was almost unbearable. I had just taken my place, on the chair nearest the pillow, when Anneke came in.

'Some of you have probably never witnessed a birth, so I will let you watch a short film, to give you some idea of what's involved.'

I noticed one of the special screens on the wall on my left and, after a few seconds, the film began.

I could see a rather frail old lady, lying on a bed, surrounded by very concerned friends and relatives. The doctor had waited until the old lady had taken her last breath. He paused for a moment, checked for a heartbeat, then announced that the loved one had departed. At that very moment I could see the old lady's soul leaving her body and trying in vain to comfort her loved ones, without success.

After a short pause the portal between here and Earth appeared. After a few moments' hesitation the old lady began her final journey, which took, in total, around 30 minutes. During this time she had the opportunity to watch an overview of her life.

Her spiritual body was already prepared, and laid out carefully on a bed, which was surrounded by friends and relatives. The scenes that followed were highly emotional. The old lady's eyes began to open and, after a few moments, she began to realize where she was. The tears of love, wonder and joy that filled the room gave us all a foretaste of what was to come.

As soon as the film ended, I turned around to look at the bed. Anneke had already prepared my father's spiritual body. It was a strange and uncanny experience, looking at the empty shell on the bed, soon to be filled by my father. The new spiritual body made my father look much younger than I could remember him.
'He should be arriving soon,' said Will, as he entered the room.
My eyes were fixed firmly on my father's face, waiting for that first moment of awakening. It came sooner than I had expected. I noticed a movement in one of my father's arms, swiftly followed by a few grunts and groans until, finally, my beloved father opened his new spiritual eyes. I do not think that words can adequately describe the emotions that were shown and felt in that room. 'Tears of joy' only scratches the surface.
Will was the first to speak, assuring my father that he wasn't dreaming and then, after making sure everything was in order, Will and Anneke left the room.

'Archie!' exclaimed my grandmother, lovingly. 'It's so good to see you again.'
My father's eyes were, by this time, glistening with tears of recognition and joy.
'How's mother?' I blurted out, unable to contain my excitement any longer.
'Oh, she's fine, as usual. We spoke at length about this moment and together made a few plans for her possible future without me. I don't think that she has ever been able to come to terms with your death, especially at such a young age, and no body to bury or funeral to mourn at. But on the whole she's a lot stronger than most people would think.'
I leaned over and kissed my father's tear-stained cheeks.
'Well,' I began, 'as you can see, I'm fine. I've got so much to show you up here. I will come and visit you in a few days, after you've rested.'
I gave my father a loving hug and, after saying goodbye to my relatives, made my way back to the reception area. I thanked Will and Anneke for their hospitality and immediately found

myself back home, looking longingly at my four-poster bed. After a short meditation, I lay down and drifted into a deep dreaming sleep, filled with the thoughts, emotions and happenings that I had just been lucky enough to witness.

I woke up some time later, feeling completely refreshed and brimming full with energy. After careful thought, I decided that it was time to change the house a little, starting with some old-fashioned gardening. Maybe I should even plant some sunflowers. My parents always adored sunflowers, I thought, visualizing the vicarage garden in full bloom. I had just finished putting in the last seed when Jen arrived, carrying something under her arm.

'I've brought you a present,' she said, smiling mischievously as she handed me a long wooden log, artistically carved and painted on the outside.

I thanked her for my surprise present and, trying not to appear too ignorant or stupid, asked her what it was.

'It's a musical instrument,' she replied and promptly began to blow into the narrowed end of the piece of wood. Almost immediately, the air was filled with the strangest and most heavenly sounds. I watched in amazement as Jen began to change her lip movements, creating new melodies. I was completely taken aback and also intrigued by the sudden change in atmosphere brought about by this instrument.

Jen explained that the instrument had been made from a eucalyptus tree, by Australian aboriginals. In time it would be used as a healing tool for various disorders. Apparently the deeply resonating musical tones produced by this remarkably simple instrument matched perfectly with the tones produced by energy centres in the human body. If used on a regular basis, the instrument cleansed the body's energy field.

Jen and I decided to go for a stroll to look at some of the newly sprouting fir trees in the valley. I was soon well into the story about my father, when I noticed a sad expression on Jen's face.

'What's the matter?' I exclaimed.

'You'd better sit down,' she said. Something in the tone of her voice made me realize that bad news was on the way.

'Well,' she began, hesitantly. 'You know that we are going to be returning to Earth again?'

'Yes.'

'Whilst I was at home resting I received a visit from my guardian angel, who told me that you would be going back quite soon and I would be following later.'

This news took me completely by surprise. I had become so immersed in my adventures that I had lost all sense of the normal time-scale. I knew that there was no escaping the fact that I would be returning to Earth once again, and that there could be no postponing the set date and time. I just didn't feel ready for the responsibilities and situations that I would no doubt encounter upon my return, although I knew they were a relevant and necessary part of my education.

Jen moved in with me immediately, so we could at least spend as much time together as possible. We spent most of that time talking, painting, walking and making imaginary plans for our future. One day, completely out of the blue, we received a visit from David, which was a nice surprise, as I hadn't seen or heard from him for a while.

'Hello, sorry to disturb you both,' he began. 'I've got some news, regarding your imminent reincarnation, Richard.'

'What sort of news?' I asked resignedly, fearing the worst.

'Well, perhaps it would be more suitable if you came to visit me for a few days. Maybe I could shed a little more light on your situation and, hopefully, allay some of your fears.'

I agreed to David's proposal and, after making arrangements, David said goodbye and left.

'Don't worry,' said Jen. 'It's not going to work out so badly. After all, we are going to meet again on Earth, in the future.'

'Yes, but when?' I replied, irritated by all the uncertainty.

'Those are some of the questions you should probably ask David. Maybe he knows the answers,' Jen replied, optimistically.

Time seemed to fly by and, before we knew it, the day of my visit to David had arrived. Jen had in the meantime already decided to return to her parents. We embraced lovingly, as Jen promised to pass on my greetings to her family.

I sat alone for a few moments in silent contemplation, trying to get things straight in my mind. The more I seemed to think, the more unanswered questions seemed to arise, until, suddenly and without warning, I found myself sitting in deep snow, surrounded on all sides by range upon range of mountains.

What now? I thought to myself, wondering why I'd been transported to this particular location. I decided to take a walk to see if I could find any answers.

The scenery was outstanding wherever I looked. The mountains had beautiful snow-covered peaks, and small grassy knolls punctuated many of the low-lying foothills. The jewel in this magnificent crown proved to be the small crystal-clear mountain streams that had melted intricate patterns and designs deep into the snow-covered mountains.

I had been walking for a short while, intent upon absorbing the spectacular scenery, when I came upon the entrance to a cave cut neatly into one of the imposing mountain-sides. I made my way slowly but cautiously towards it, not knowing what to expect. As I neared the opening to the cave, I could hear a faint noise wafting out. Men chanting, I thought, deciding to turn around and continue my journey.

'Richard!' shouted a strangely dressed man, who had suddenly appeared at the entrance. 'Welcome. We've been expecting you.'

Not again, I thought, wondering why all these coincidental meetings were arranged without my knowledge.

'Follow me,' said the man, who seemed to be a monk, from some religious order. I followed the shaven-headed, orange-clad figure until we reached the end of the dimly lit cave.

Suddenly the whole of this subterranean cavern was illuminated. The intense light felt like a thousand Earth suns, shining simultaneously. I realized now where the chanting had come from. Eleven shaven-headed monks, all neatly dressed in orange robes, sat in a circle on the cave floor.

My guide introduced himself as John, and began to explain that the monks who sat on the cave floor were spiritual guides. They were in almost-continual contact with spiritual leaders and other spiritually advanced people on Earth. He was to be my spiritual contact while I was on Earth.

He continued to explain, in great detail, the many forms of contact that could be achieved between the two dimensions, especially during deep meditation and, as was more usual, while dreaming.

'Sometimes if a particular person has strayed far away from

their spiritual path, we arrange for an accident to occur, so that the soul can be temporarily dislodged from its body, enabling us to communicate directly with the individual, who is then allowed to return to the body to continue their education in a higher state of awareness than previously. Scientists and doctors on earth have been studying this phenomenon but have been unable to come up with any sort of satisfactory explanation for this occurrence, although when the time is ripe this knowledge will be made available.

'If, at any time, you feel the need for guidance or help in spiritual matters, you may communicate directly with me,' concluded John solemnly, adding that I would receive the necessary information regarding meditation after my 28th year on Earth.

'Why only after 28 years?' I asked, puzzled.

'Because this time will signal a spiritual rebirth within you. This is also one of the universal laws. Every seven years your body, spiritual as well as physical, undergoes a complete change which makes the contact between the two dimensions easier and more accessible.'

He paused momentarily, giving me a chance to try to assimilate this extra information.

'After this change in consciousness, you will become much more spiritually aware and this will enable you to perform what most people on Earth would regard as miracles.'

I sat down on the cave floor, watching intently as, one by one, each of the monks communicated their spiritual information to their contacts on Earth. I could see many different people, from all walks of life and many cultures, deep in meditation, thus enabling the contact to run a much smoother path. The people on Earth didn't seem to be aware of the fact that their spiritual body had loosened itself from the physical and was actually travelling to communicate more directly with their spiritual guides. The people probably thought that the trip was just a part of their meditational experience, but the cave, the monks and their information were very real indeed.

I thanked my future spiritual guide and began to retrace my steps along the cave. I had just reached the halfway point, when the scenery began to fade and, in a whirlwind of speed and colour, I found myself standing on one of the highest peaks in this incredible mountain range. To my surprise, the area surrounding me seemed to be completely flat with here and there a light sprinkling of powdery snow. In the distance, I could see my eventual destination, an enormous transparent pyramid, surrounded by myriad gardens, footpaths and forests. I decided to walk to the pyramid, not wishing to miss one sight or sound in this heavenly creation.

The fantastic paradise seemed to be full of wildlife. I watched in fascination as a pride of lions browsed on the lush green leaves of a tropical plant, while totally ignoring a passing herd of zebras. Birds of all shapes and sizes flitted in and out of the trees, singing the most haunting melodies I'd ever heard and, last but not least, I even caught a glimpse of the mythical unicorn!

As I made my way through this magical landscape, towards the pyramid, I saw that David was waiting for me. This time I'd known that he would be there to greet me. I was, at last, learning to listen to my intuition and to trust it.

'Welcome to my home!' David greeted me. 'Come in.'

After following him along countless corridors and passing many doors and entrances, David led me into a brightly illuminated, triangular-shaped room.

'Now, sit yourself down and make yourself at home. This is the closest you have come so far to our Creator. Rest for a while and try to adapt to the atmosphere.'

An overpowering feeling of forgiveness, love and understanding surged through me, as my consciousness was raised by our Creator. I looked around, as David departed into one of the smaller anterooms. The room, with its distinctively triangular form, had been constructed entirely out of glass, apart from the soft padded wool floor. Where is the furniture? I thought, walking towards the window.

The view outside was magnificent surpassing anything else I had seen. In the sky there were tens of thousands of stars and many planets, shining with an intensity only reserved, I believe, for newly created planets. I watched in awe the countless minuscule specks of light, travelling at breakneck speed towards the various planets and finally disappearing from sight, as they entered the planet's atmosphere.

Intuitively, I understood what was taking place. The flashes of light were new souls, incarnating on the newly created planets. Our Creator did not stop after the creation of our own solar system. The creation continues, unabated.

Every question I formulated was immediately answered, although the answers seemed to originate in my own intuition. My consciousness had been raised to such a level that the need for further questioning became redundant. The secrets of the entire universe were within me, and always had been. I had just come to terms with this astonishing fact when David reappeared and asked me to go with him.

Following him into a much smaller side room, I noticed one of the special walls, where the three-dimensional films were shown.

'Now,' began David, matter of factly. 'Take your time, and if you should have any further questions, I will be glad to answer them.'

I sat down on the comfortable padded floor and the film began. The first scene showed a man and woman living completely separate lives. They eventually met, fell in love and got married. The woman had lived in a large family and went to church regularly, until, slowly but surely, she realized that the teachings of the Church had no bearing on the reality of her own life. Some of the circumstances of her life would move her further and further away from the Church and its teachings. This would be due to the tragedies that would occur within her family.

The second sequence concentrated on the man who lived in a smaller family. His upbringing was a traditional one; he was taught to respect everyone and also that hard work would eventually bring about its rewards. He had a heart of gold, and was quite spiritually advanced, on an unconscious level. I watched, intrigued, as the couple's individual spiritual guides planted different ideas and notions into their subconscious minds, in an effort to bring the couple together. Finally, their two paths crossed. Such matters were viewed entirely as coincidental on Earth. The fact is that all coincidences have their own special meaning.

The two strangers were to be my new parents. Once again I would be born in England. I was shown my place of birth, the exact dates and time, and told how this would affect my future incarnation. I was also shown the attributes and character that I would be taking with me, along with some of the experiences I could expect.

A new spiritual age was dawning on Earth, with many of the spiritually advanced souls incarnating simultaneously. Many scientists and professors would be forced to re-think their outdated theories, especially concerning the creation of the Earth. There were also the seemingly endless possibilities of the human consciousness and, last but not least, environmental issues would come to the fore, after being ignored for too long.

I watched a newsreel, showing strange shapes appearing in fields of standing corn, usually overnight. These strange phenomena would herald a great change and a leap of consciousness on Earth, forcing its inhabitants to think again about their way of life.

The planet Earth has its own consciousness and after decades of pollution and general misuse was beginning to cleanse itself. I could see many fatalities, due mainly to earthquakes, volcanic eruptions and a drastic change in the weather. New political groups were forming to protest against the testing of nuclear weapons. Not only did these release deadly radiation but the shock waves from such an enormous blasts caused tremors and earthquakes and, gravest of all, affected the tilt of the Earth's axis. This created danger for our own future generations and also for the inhabitants of other planets within our solar system, the very existence of whom challenged mankind's egotistical views about the universe.

I could see clearly the shock waves reaching other more advanced civilizations who, mainly out of concern for their own planets, began to organize themselves into various groups which visited Earth on a regular basis, in an effort to convince the people of the error of their ways.

I was also shown a programme of interbreeding between advanced beings and specially selected humans, the aim of which was to enable stability, peace and love to reign upon Earth.

Most of the universal laws became much clearer while watching the film. The thing that struck me most of all was the fact that each individual on Earth was linked inextricably with every other. Our actions, thoughts and deeds affected others and this resulted in a sort of ripple effect, which stretched around the entire planet and eventually returned much amplified, to its originator.

Towards the end of the film I was allowed a brief oversight of my new life. A flood of love, warmth and understanding pulsed through my consciousness as I realized that Alison was going to be my sister and Juliette would have a significant part to play later on in my life. Some of the situations seemed to be a little on the harsh side, especially concerning my relationships and marriage, but I had been assured that one could learn far more from a difficult situation than an easy one.

The film ended abruptly, leaving me once again staring at a blank wall as David walked in.

'Well, what did you think?' he prompted.

I remained silent, completely lost in thought about my new life, especially the more unpleasant aspects.

'Oh, there's nothing to worry about,' said David. 'If you need any guidance I will always be there to help you, no matter how difficult the situation appears. All you have to do is meditate in the manner you have been shown. If you forget how to meditate, I will make sure that you come across the information, while you are on Earth.'

David's words calmed me down. We began to talk about spiritual matters and the whys and wherefores concerning our many lives upon the Earth, until Jen's voice interrupted our conversation.

'Go on, Richard. I will see you again shortly before you make your final journey.'

I just managed to thank David, before I arrived outside my home, where Jen and my father were waiting to greet me. Quickly I had relayed the whole adventure to my father and Jen, as we ambled lazily through the countryside. During our walk my father explained that he would soon be moving on.

'Moving on? Where to?' I asked in surprise.

'Well, Richard, as you yourself have seen, there are many more spheres of existence. That's why your grandparents were able to be here to greet me. They are now passing on their earthly knowledge to new souls, prior to their first incarnation on Earth.'

I cut him short, saying that I would just like to share these last moments, enjoying his company without complicating matters further. We spent the rest of the time together, looking at the scenery and reminiscing about my mother and some of the fantastic times we had spent together on Earth, as a family. At the end of the day, Jen and I waved a tearful goodbye to my father, who assured me that one day we would all meet up again.

Jen and I spent a long time changing the house and its surrounding scenery until we were both satisfied. I tried not to dwell too much on the future, choosing instead to adorn our house with as many paintings as I could before my departure. Jen had decided to remain in the house until her own time arrived.

I didn't have too long to wait, as an intense feeling of dread and doom became more and more apparent, until the day came when David arrived.

'It's time, Richard.'

Jen and I fell into one another's arms, in floods of tears and sorrow. I hadn't been able to come to terms with the fact that I would have to leave Jen behind. After a brief talk with David, it was agreed that Jen could accompany us to the reincarnation centre.

At David's request the three of us held hands. I just managed to catch a last fleeting glimpse of our home, and its heavenly surroundings, before we arrived in a large waiting room. Jen and I sat down together, whilst David asked one of the assistants which room had been allocated. After a brief discussion, we were led through a dimly lit labyrinth of corridors, until we had reached our final destination.

The room itself was also dimly lit, sparsely furnished with a bed and several comfortable-looking chairs. I walked over to the other side of the room to glance out of the window. There it was, the Earth in all its glory, surrounded by a bright blue aura, the colour of which corresponded with the fifth human energy centre. I stared in wonder at my destination, realizing immediately that the Earth had been through many energy changes since its creation. With each of man's rises in consciousness the aura surrounding the earth would reflect these changes. I was just thinking about the next leap in man's consciousness when a fair-haired, white-coated assistant arrived. She quickly explained the simple procedure. All I had to do was to lie down on the bed and relax. I hugged Jen tearfully, saying a last sad goodbye until we met again. Only the next time it would be under very different circumstances.

David explained that most of my memories of this place would be hidden, until a certain point in my life. He added that he would always be there to guide and help me, should I feel the need.

I took one last look at Jen's tear-stained face, before finally climbing on to the bed. The assistant walked over to the bed, carrying a thin white cotton cloth, which she placed carefully over my eyes. Within an instant everything became dark. The next moment, I was hurtling at breakneck speed through a spiral tunnel of darkness which seemed to go on for ever and ever . . .

FOURTEEN

I had at last received my hidden memories, confirming every-thing I'd known concerning our human evolution and the part we play in our own universe. I must have read these chapters over a hundred times and still couldn't believe that I myself had written them, although I knew that the information was the absolute truth.

Jennifer soon brought me back down to earth by reminding me that I still had the unenviable task of finding a publisher. After buying the current *Writer's Handbook* I began to check through the varying publishing houses until coming across the entry for Element Books, whose avowed publishing policy was 'to make available knowledge and information to aid humanity in a time of major transition'.

This is it, I thought to myself, deciding immediately to write a covering letter and synopsis and send a completed chapter to Element to gauge their interest. I didn't for one moment dream that I would receive a positive reply, considering how many potential writers could paper their walls with letters of rejection.

One week later I received what I thought would be my own letter of rejection and couldn't believe my eyes after I'd torn open the envelope. 'Dear Martin, thank you for your enquiry regarding your proposed book. Please could you send the completed manuscript with a view to publication?' Jennifer congratulated me on my extremely good luck and we decided to go out for a celebratory meal that very same night.

The next day I was overwhelmed with thoughts of doom and failure. What if Element rejected my completed manuscript?

I thought, and in the end I decided to go through the *Writer's Handbook* once again, just in case I had missed any other potential publishers. I was about to put the book down when I came across an interesting entry in the magazine section. *Reincarnation International*, the only magazine in the world dealing with all aspects of reincarnation. What a coincidence, I thought to myself, smiling wryly as I carefully typed out a letter to the editor explaining my particular story concerning reincarnation. I wondered how my story would compare with other accounts from around the world. I knew that not only was my story true, I also had the means to prove it once and for all. I carefully inserted a copy of the crash report in the letter and on the short walk to the post office remembered with relief my decision to have the sessions with the aura reader and the regression therapist recorded on tape. I had even kept the collectors' magazine in which I found the hobbyist's address; all of this material would be necessary I felt, if my story was to be taken seriously.

I received quite a positive letter of reply from Roy Stemman, the editor of *Reincarnation International*. He thanked me for taking the time and trouble to write to the magazine and explained that, though he found my story fascinating and although he could not provide me with any financial reward, he hoped that I would write a more detailed account for his magazine, adding that it would probably lead to a few enquiries from the press, radio or television.

I hadn't thought for one moment that my story would be interesting enough for a magazine, let alone the television, although the publicity would come in handy for my book.

As I was writing my reply to Roy, I suddenly remembered a television series about the paranormal in Holland and after checking on the teletext and making a note of the programme's postal address I wrote a brief account of the happenings since I'd moved to Holland, adding that I would be willing to be interviewed for the programme.

I'd almost forgotten about my letters until during one morning's work on my book the telephone rang. Who could this be? I wondered, more than a little annoyed at the distraction. My initial annoyance soon turned to excitement – a researcher from the paranormal programme had read my letter and wanted to arrange an interview with me at their head office just outside Hilversum. After checking my diary I arranged to meet her early in the New Year.

The day of my appointment with the television company arrived and after double-checking that I'd packed the evidence to back up my story I caught the train to Bussum. I was full of nervous excitement, wondering about the very real possibility that I would have to tell my story in front of the television cameras.

After being offered a cup of strong Dutch coffee I made myself comfortable in the waiting room and was just about to pick one of the magazines off the table as the research assistant arrived. After brief introductions I followed her upstairs into her office and the interview began immediately. I tried my best to get a word in as the barrage of questions continued. After two exhausting hours it became clear to me that the company was very interested in my story, although the researcher informed me at the end of our interview that she would have to dig deeper into my story and asked me if I had any objections to their research in England.

'None at all,' I replied, rather naïvely.

'Yes, but you must bear in mind that there is a possibility that we may come into contact with one of Richard's relatives,' cautioned the assistant. 'How would you feel about that, Martin?'

'I will cross that bridge when and if we come to it,' I replied, though I felt more than a little uneasy at the prospect.

'Any other questions, Martin?'

'Yes, as a matter of fact, I have one question. Will you be travelling to the vicarage in England to check out any of the details I recalled whilst under hypnosis?'

My thoughts were more than a little confused on the journey home, especially after reviewing the assistant's reply to my last question. She would do her best to acquire as much information concerning Richard's life as possible over the telephone, and 'maybe' they would eventually send a film crew to the vicarage. I was more than a little dissatisfied with her reply, although I resigned myself to the prospect. After all, she was the expert.

My meeting with the television company was soon forgotten as I resumed the difficult task of continuing with writing my book. Any sort of social life that I'd managed to build up had slowly diminished to a meeting or telephone call now and again. I was extremely thankful to my understanding acquaintances and friends, who gave me all the support and encouragement that I would need in the coming months.

I had just finished speaking to my old colleague and friend Mary and had replaced the telephone on its cradle when it began to ring, startling me momentarily. It was the researcher from the television company who asked me if I had my RAF service number and dates of service and that the information was urgently needed for their ongoing research. I quickly located the relevant information and after carefully spelling out the names of the bases I'd been stationed at I asked the researcher why she needed this particular information.

'Well, we've been quite busy researching into your case, Martin, but at this point in time I don't wish to reveal too much. I promise I will contact you later on this week if your information checks out correctly.'

Of course it will check out correctly, I thought, wondering what on earth she was up to.

The answer came a few days later when she telephoned me to ask if I had any objections to undergoing another regression. After agreeing to this, I gave her Josee's telephone number so that she could organize a date for my second regression. The assistant then told me that she had a surprise in store for me concerning Richard and his family, and that she would reveal all after the regression.

The following few days were very frustrating for me. I couldn't seem to concentrate fully on my book and my imagination was working overtime trying to work out what sort of surprise could be in store for me. Then first Josee and then the assistant telephoned me to check that the following Wednesday morning would be a suitable day for my second regression. This time it will be different, very different, I thought to myself, going over the assistant's words once more in my mind.

'We will be filming the regression, Martin, with your permission of course.'

I consented immediately – after all I had nothing to hide. My only worry was whether I would be able to relax enough under the glare of the television cameras to reach the level needed to be successfully regressed.

*   *   *

Any worries I'd had concerning relaxation soon melted, as I sat listening to Josee's hauntingly hypnotic voice. She explained her procedure to the television assistant downstairs, while the camera and sound crews were busy setting up their equipment in one of the spare bedrooms. Ten minutes later I lay on a massage table being made up and fitted with a microphone. The light from the television camera was exceptionally strong, although I had the luxury of being able to close my eyes, unlike Josee, I thought. My eyelids closed ready for her hypnotic induction speech.

As far as I could remember the words were exactly the same as the first time. Within no time at all, and despite the thoughts about the intrusion of camera and crew, my body relaxed. The next moment I'd been transported back in time and had ended up outside the vicarage, standing in the garden at the back. What a fantastic feeling, I thought as I stared at the beautifully kept garden with its ornamental fountain; the sun was shining brightly as the birds were singing in total harmony with nature. I'd just started to get so carried away with this sudden lease of freedom that I'd completely forgotten my main reason for returning. Then Josee's distant voice interrupted the idyllic scene, asking me to describe what I was seeing. It took me a great deal of effort to communicate with this intruder's voice. Where is the voice coming from? I thought as I grudgingly followed its instructions.

Two hours later my trip down memory lane was completed when Josee brought me back to consciousness, totally against my will. I had felt so peaceful and relaxed where I'd been and here I was once again back in my extremely heavy body, suddenly realizing an urgent need to go to the toilet, although I would have to wait for ten minutes before I regained full control of my body movements.

Josee congratulated me on my performance in front of the television camera and the television assistant said that she would contact me later on in the week, when the film had been processed.

'Yes, but what about my surprise?' I blurted out.

'Oh, that.' The assistant explained that she had contacted Richard's only remaining relative, his brother-in-law, who had agreed, together with his son, to cooperate fully and provide as much information as they could remember about Richard's life.

Apparently Richard had had three sisters and the assistant wanted to find out if I could name them. I remembered Josee asking me on more than one occasion during the regression if there was anybody else in the house apart from my parents and on both occasions I replied negatively.

'Listen,' began Josee, realizing by the look on my face that I was disappointed. 'I explained what you can and can't expect from hypnotic regression to the assistant; I told her that what you are seeing is just one moment in time and that if she wanted more specific information it would take more sessions. After all this is only your second regression. For most people it would take many more sessions to acquire even a small fraction of the information that you have managed to recall.'

I arrived home in a state of utter confusion, wondering why I'd not seen any of Richard's sisters, especially as I'd recalled far more details concerning various other points in Richard's life. Doubt began to well up in my mind. Maybe everything I'd seen under regression was simply my imagination and the fact that I'd known Richard's name, his age, occupation and his father's occupation as a vicar was sheer coincidence.

I relayed the day's events to Jennifer, including a description of the village where Richard had lived. The pictures were real enough, I thought, describing the beautiful river that ran through the village, including a rather picturesque bridge near where Richard used to go fishing. There was a small row of shops for the villagers and the church where Richard's father was the incumbent had a short spire. I found this rather strange, as most of the churches in England that I could remember had tall spires.

'Anything else?' prompted Jennifer.

'The village square had a strange-shaped monument that didn't seem to fit in with the rest of the scenery.'

'It's no coincidence,' she reassured me, after listening to my story concerning Richard's sisters. Don't forget, you even know that Richard's body would not be found, as it was destroyed in the explosion.'

'I suppose so,' I mumbled, downhearted.

Two days later the researcher telephoned to organize a second interview for the following week, explaining that they would like to film me working on my book, along with various other locations in Hoorn, including the library where I'd coincidentally found the collectors' magazine.

Jennifer and I spent the weekend cleaning and tidying the house in preparation for my big day. Most of the day before the interview was spent on checking and double-checking all the bits and pieces of information. I was just about to start preparing the evening meal when the telephone began to ring. After a short conversation I flopped down on to the settee, with a mixture of stunned disappointment and anger. The television company had decided not to film my story after all.

'I will explain everything tomorrow,' the researcher assured me.

A dark cloud of depression hung over the evening meal, as Jennifer and I speculated endlessly as to the reason for such a last-minute cancellation.

'Well, whatever the reason, it's their loss,' said Jennifer, asking me to telephone her at work the following day, after the research assistant had left.

The young woman explained her research in great detail, adding that their decision to discontinue work on my case was due mainly in the fact that I'd failed to see that Richard had three sisters. I interrupted her diatribe to ask her about all the other things I'd seen, not to mention the coincidences, facts and details.

'That is a great mystery, Martin,' was her reply.

Before she left she handed me a large buff envelope containing all the research material. 'Please let me know how your book gets on,' she added, walking towards her car.

I closed the front door and hurried up the stairs, eager to read what she had discovered during her research.

She had made contact with Richard's brother-in-law and explained briefly what my story entailed and asked for his cooperation regarding Richard's life. The man himself was quite old and told the assistant that his son knew everything about Richard and would cooperate with her inquiries.

After transcribing the text from the second regression the assistant had constructed a list of pointed questions, which she then sent to Richard's nephew. He then read the questions and marked 'yes' or 'no' answers on the list. I couldn't believe my eyes; out of the whole list only 15 questions had been answered and out of the 15, five of my observations whilst under regression were proved to be indisputably correct. I ended up going around in circles for the rest of that frustrating afternoon.

After carefully scrutinizing the list I'd realized that if Richard's nephew could answer one particular question, then he should have been able to answer one of the more obvious questions. My blood began to boil when I read the section entitled 'Richard and the RAF'. The assistant had written: 'I will not tell the details about what he did and how he died, since Martin could have known that from his own RAF service.'

'She either did not believe my story, or she had not taken me seriously enough,' I said to Jennifer, who by this time was studying the contents of the buff envelope.

'She should have asked open questions,' muttered Jennifer. 'You would have received an unbiased result in that case.' She was doing her utmost to cheer me up. 'Well, you will just have to continue writing your book. Something will come up, I'm sure.'

Several sleepless nights later I was even considering stopping writing. After all, what's the point? I thought, although somewhere deep down inside me I knew that everything I'd been witness to under regression, along with the unbelievable happenings and coincidences in my life would not be in vain. Jennifer insisted that I continue with my book, despite this one setback. I agreed to start writing again after my birthday, which was less than a week away.

Jennifer had already organized a visit to her parents in England on my birthday and Mary invited me to spent the night with her and her boyfriend in Amsterdam. I accepted Mary's invitation and had just put the telephone down when it began to ring again.

'Hello Martin, it's Roy Stemman from *Reincarnation International* here!'

We had a pleasant chat and then Roy told me that he would be in Amsterdam for two days next week and asked if I had time to do an interview. I accepted Roy's offer and he gave me the telephone number of the hotel where he would be staying. He had telephoned them for the address, but couldn't understand the Dutch accent.

I thanked Roy for his interest and marked the time and date in my diary, deciding to telephone the hotel the following Monday.

'I told you something would come up,' said Jennifer wryly, after I'd told her about my conversation with Roy.

*   *   *

The next day I helped her to pack and accompanied her to the airport, waving a final emotional goodbye as she passed through passport control. I was certainly going to miss her, although she would only be gone for a long weekend.

I soon arrived back home in Hoorn and began to prepare my evening meal when Mary telephoned to tell me which tram number I would have to catch the following day.

As arranged, Mary was waiting for me at the tram terminus.

'Hello stranger,' she said, jokingly. 'How does it feel to be twenty-one again?'

On the way to the flat we decided to pick up a Chinese meal for the evening.

'Where's Peter?' I enquired, wondering why she'd only ordered for two people.

'Oh, he's gone to meet one of his friends who – coincidentally – has found temporary work in a hotel not far from here.'

'That's handy,' I replied, laughing at Mary's sarcastic tone. 'Which hotel?'

'The Piet Heijn.'

'Never heard of it.'

'I'm not surprised, there must be thousands of hotels in Amsterdam,' and Mary poured a generous amount of red wine into my glass. We spent the rest of the evening catching up on all the gossip, and reminiscing about our time at the CD company.

'Good luck with your interview next week,' Mary shouted as I was boarding the train for Hoorn. I'd almost forgotten about my meeting with Roy, and decided to telephone the hotel the following morning to ask for directions, before going back to the airport to meet Jennifer.

'Good morning, Piet Heijn hotel.'

'Sorry, could you repeat that please?' I stammered, scarcely believing what I'd just heard.

'Piet Heijn hotel, can I help you?'

Mary's words echoed around in my mind as the receptionist explained which tram route I should take from the Central Station. 'There must be thousands of hotels in Amsterdam!'

A warm glow of satisfaction enveloped my being as the realization hit me that, despite my disappointing experience with the television company, coincidence had, for the umpteenth time, created another opportunity.

Jennifer showed no hint of surprise after I'd told her about the coincidence.

'You don't have to prove anything to me, Martin. I already know,' she said, wishing me good luck for my meeting with Roy.

I arrived in the hotel foyer ten minutes early for our appointment. The receptionist telephoned Roy for me and he came down to the foyer to meet me.

'Hello, Martin, pleased to meet you in the flesh at last,' said the smiling middle-aged man.

Ten minutes later the interview began in earnest. Following a barrage of questions and answers I presented Roy with copies of all the documents relevant to my case, including the research papers from the television company.

'Well, you've heard the evidence, Roy. What do you think?'

He paused for a moment, as if gathering his thoughts.

'Well Martin, if you want my honest opinion, I've worked on a number of quite famous reincarnation cases over the years, and yours has the potential to become just as well known. I have quite a few contacts in the media. How would you feel about a television programme?'

My heart sank as I explained to Roy the disappointing experience I'd just undergone with the Dutch television company.

'Oh, don't worry about that I know just the kind of programme that will treat your case with the utmost sincerity. Have you heard of the series *Strange But True*?'

'Which channel?'

'Ah, you only receive BBC over here. Well it's made by London Weekend Television, although I must admit I haven't heard anything from them in a long while.

'Tell you what,' he went on, after seeing the reluctant look on my face. 'I will give you a couple of weeks to make up your mind. How about that?'

I agreed to Roy's proposal. After all, I could always say no. Following a hasty photo session outside the hotel, Roy and I called in to one of the many street cafes in Amsterdam for breakfast and a coffee. I explained the great role that coincidence had played during my life and the remarkable coincidence concerning Roy's hotel, adding that sometimes these so-called coincidences affected other people who'd had contact with me. The expression on Roy's face told me that he had some difficulty in believing me and as our meeting came to an end, Roy handed me his home telephone number and asked me to inform him of my decision regarding the television series within two weeks. I promised to get back to him and after shaking his hand, I jokingly added, 'Don't forget to look out for coincidences!'

'I understand your disappointment, but think about the publicity,' said Jennifer that same evening.

I agreed. 'The publicity will be good for the book, but I just don't want to end up in the same situation as before – once bitten, twice shy.'

'Well, it's entirely up to you and, anyway, you have got two weeks to make up your mind, so don't forget.'

The next morning I arose early, determined to make a good start on my book and noticed that there was a message on the answering machine.

'Hello, Martin, Roy Stemman speaking. You probably won't believe this, but when I arrived home last night there was a message on my answering machine from the programme *Strange But True*. Could you telephone me back as soon as possible?'

Well, he'll believe me now, I thought, as I dialled Roy's number.

Apparently a case that *Strange But True* were working on had fallen through at the very last minute. They had contacted Roy to see if he had any interesting cases for them.

'They were very excited about your case and want to interview you in Holland. What do you think?'

I agreed to the interview without hesitation and reminded Roy about our conversation concerning coincidences.

'Yes, that is very strange,' said Roy, promising to ring me back as soon as he'd organized the interview.

Twenty minutes later I received a telephone call from Carlton Black, one of the producers from the programme, asking me for more details regarding my case. The interview itself came two days later when Carlton and his assistant flew over to Holland to speak to some of the people involved in my story. Eventually it was decided that Josee, Jennifer and I would fly to London the following week for filming.

The day itself finally arrived and I must admit to being more than a little nervous. After all, this was to be my first live interview.

Josee, Jennifer and I were in our hotel room drinking coffee when the film crew arrived, to be followed by Roy, who told me that one of Carlton's assistants had visited Swallowfield and apparently everything I'd seen under hypnosis fitted perfectly, including the picturesque river which runs through the village, the church with its unusual short spire, a pretty bridge over the river and, last but not least, an interview with one of the village historians, who pointed out the vicarage as it stands today, which didn't match the description I'd given. The assistant added that the vicarage had been two doors away during the war years; my description of 'my' vicarage fitted this other house exactly!

Three hours later the interviews were complete and following a lunch at the hotel the television company promised to send me a copy of the completed video and wished us all good luck. The return flight seemed to pass me by completely. Roy's words concerning Swallowfield were haunting my mind. Once again coincidence had thrown me a lifeline, just when I was about to give up my quest and throw in the towel.

Jennifer and I promised to keep in contact with Josee and let her know if there were any further developments.

I continued to work on my book for four months until one day the video finally arrived. Jennifer was working so I had to watch it on my own. I sat down in nervous anticipation, wondering how my story would come across. Michael Aspel, the presenter, introduced the programme and 15 emotional minutes later there I sat, scarcely able to believe what I had just seen.

The television company had reconstructed my story using actors with the interviews being shown in between the re-enacted events. The film confirmed all my claims as to what I had seen and experienced under regression. During the final few minutes when the footage of Swallowfield began, tears of recognition streamed down my cheeks. I seemed to be temporarily caught up in some kind of strange time continuum in which the 1930s became the 1990s and vice versa.

I lay down and closed my eyes. The realization had just dawned on me – my destiny had been fulfilled.